# He Listened to Us

# He Listened to Us

## A Maya Witness to
## Blessed Stanley "Apla's" Rother

—⚬

JUAN AJTZIP

As told to and translated by GERALD W. SCHLABACH, editor
With a foreword by CARDINAL ÁLVARO LEONEL RAMAZZINI

RESOURCE *Publications* · Eugene, Oregon

HE LISTENED TO US
A Maya Witness to Blessed Stanley "Apla's" Rother

Copyright © 2025 Gerald Schlabach. All rights reserved. Except for brief quotations in critical publications or reviews, no part of this book may be reproduced in any manner without prior written permission from the publisher. Write: Permissions, Wipf and Stock Publishers, 199 W. 8th Ave., Suite 3, Eugene, OR 97401.

Resource Publications
An Imprint of Wipf and Stock Publishers
199 W. 8th Ave., Suite 3
Eugene, OR 97401

www.wipfandstock.com

PAPERBACK ISBN: 979-8-3852-5451-4
HARDCOVER ISBN: 979-8-3852-5452-1
EBOOK ISBN: 979-8-3852-5453-8

## *Cataloguing-in-Publication data:*

Names: Ajtzip, Juan. | Edited and translated by Gerald W. Schlabach. | Foreword by Cardinal Alvaro Leonel Ramazzini.

Title: He listened to us : a Maya witness to Blessed Stanley "Apla's" Rother / Gerald Schlabach.

Description: Eugene, OR: Resource Publications, 2025 | Includes bibliographical references.

Identifiers: ISBN 979-8-3852-5451-4 (paperback) | ISBN 979-8-3852-5452-1 (hardcover) | ISBN 979-8-3852-5453-8 (ebook) | LCCN: 2025919479

Subjects: LCSH: Rother, Stanley, 1935–1981. | Catholic Church — Guatemala — Clergy — Biography. | Christian martyrs — Guatemala — Biography. | Guatemala—History—Civil War, 1960–1996 | Santiago Atitlán (Guatemala)—Religious life and customs | Missionaries — Guatemala — Biography. | Human rights—Guatemala—History—20th century

Classification: BX4705.R675 2025 (print) | BX4705 2025 (ebook)

First published as Juan Ajtzip and Gerald Schlabach (editor), *Nos escuchó: Un testimonio maya al Beato Stanley "Apla's" Rother*, foreword by Cardinal Álvaro Ramazzini Imeri (Guatemala, Guatemala: F&G Editores, 2025)

Direct scripture quotation is from the Revised Standard Version Bible: Catholic Edition, copyright © 1989, 1993 National Council of the Churches of Christ in the United States of America. Used by permission. All rights reserved worldwide.

*Cover credit: Cover photo by Sean Sprague (Alamy Stock Photo)*

Blessed Father Stanley "Apla's" Rother blesses a dinner with twelve "apostles" in preparation for the Holy Thursday mass, in which the priest acts in Jesus' place by washing their feet. (Courtesy of the Archives of the Archdiocese of Oklahoma City.)

For myself I am a Christian.
For the sake of others I am a Priest.

FATHER STANLEY FRANCIS ROTHER
Ordination card
25 May 1963

The time is past, if indeed it was ever present, when the Church could stake out a mission in unknown territory and proceed to ignore the native genius of the people whom she evangelized. Today the Church wishes to listen as well as to speak. It is a lesson of history. She speaks the message of eternal salvation, but she is not deaf to the cries of social justice which break from the throats of the underprivileged of the world. . . .

The Christian "renewal" of the people of Santiago Atitlán must come through a "dialogue" with them—the "have nots." There is much that we can learn from them. Christ hides himself in them and waits for us. We hope that our missionary work among them will result in a more resplendent revelation of Christ, both in them and in ourselves.

BISHOP VICTOR REED
Bishop of Oklahoma City
commissioning mass for
Oklahoma Catholic Mission, 1963

# Contents

# CONTENTS

# Foreword

*Cardinal Álvaro Leonel Ramazzini*
*Bishop of the Diocese*
*of Huehuetenango, Guatemala*

I HAVE READ THIS book by the teacher Juan Ajtzip, a native of the town of Santiago Atitlán here in Guatemala. The protagonists, apart from the author of the book, are the people of Santiago and their martyred parish priest, Blessed Father Stanley Rother, whom they called Padre Apla's, which means "Francis" in the Tz'utujil language.

Throughout my reading, I have discovered historical aspects that complement and reaffirm the data offered by *Guatemala, Never Again!*, the official report of the Human Rights Office of the Archdiocese of Guatemala (REMHI). This first conclusion guarantees the historical dimension of what Juan Ajtzip has told us.

I propose—and anyone who reads the book will be able to draw their own conclusions—some relevant aspects of this story.

The enormous strength of the people of Santiago Atitlán is evident, born of a consistent unity among its inhabitants, regardless of social status, religion, or political tendency. The famous slogan "Only the people save the people" is demonstrated by the attitude of solidarity by all of Santiago when facing a situation of attack against the population by the Guatemalan army.

The testimony of Father Stanley Francis Rother stands out as exemplary and consistent, for he shared the life and death of the people he served with the soul of a good shepherd. This testimony demonstrates a profound attitude of fidelity, even to the point of surrendering his own life.

Through the testimony of Juan Ajtzip, we discover the positive impact that the presence of the missionaries from the Archdiocese of Oklahoma, in the United States, had on the community of Santiago. Its effects reached beyond the strictly Catholic sphere. They were sealed with the blood of

Blessed Father Stanley and reaffirmed by the presence of the subsequent pastor, Father Thomas McSherry.

This firsthand testimony by Juan Ajtzip, growing out of his personal experience as a committed Christian, gives the book a flavor of irrefutable authenticity. Combined with the lessons we may deduce from the narrative, Ajtzip's testimony will help the reader to better understand the historical and religious significance of a people that today must continue to face the social, cultural, and religious changes of our time.

Meanwhile, I would like to reaffirm some aspects of this testimony by way of conclusion, which directly touch upon the person and actions of Juan Ajtzip.

I am struck by his life experiences amid a suffering, impoverished childhood, painfully marked by child labor on the farms of the southern coast of Guatemala, yet sheltered and protected by the presence of his parents and grandparents. They always took care of him, and in a special way, in moments of danger to his life, they defended and cared for him.

The positive influence of the exemplary life of Father Stanley Francis Rother is very evident. Throughout his life, Juan Ajtzip was strongly influenced by the life and example of Padre Apla's, who helped him grow in his personality and in the experience of his faith, forming him to live out a radical commitment to his people, following in Rother's footsteps.

At the same time, we see the growth of Juan Ajtzip's social conscience as he became convinced of the need to work for his own people and even put his life at risk during his time as director of the radio station "*La Voz de Atitlán*." This characteristic is evident in his commitment to the radio during his tenure as its director for 24 years. It is also evident in his social commitment, in which the worldview of his ancestors, and the difficult history he had to face, shaped his spirit and his heart.

A fact that should not go unnoticed is the critical and objective attention that this book devotes to the problem of transculturation in Santiago Atitlán, and its relationship with the evangelizing processes. It is worth reflecting on this analysis in the face of the religious situation that the people of Santiago Atitlán are living today.

Finally, I was powerfully struck by the sentence with which the book concludes: "But they do not listen to us."

This leaves a question mark on my conscience: What does Juan Ajtzip want to tell us?

# Acknowledgments

I WANT TO EXPRESS my gratitude for the opportunity to write the story of this priest who came to work in our community, Father Stanley Francis Rother. Thanks to his positive impact on the Maya Tz'utujil people, and our love for him, we soon began to call him by the Tz'utujil translation of his middle name, Padre Apla's. Now, in recognition for giving his life in Christian and pastoral service, the Church names him Blessed.

It has now been 43 years since the death of Blessed Father Apla's, who so loved all the children, young people, old men and women in this town and all the other communities on the shores of Lake Atitlán. Showing true Christian love through his concrete service, he left the whole Church an example of faithful pastoral priesthood. First of all, then, I want to say, "Thank you, Padre Apla's."

I am enormously grateful to the friend who has worked so hard on this editorial project, Gerald Schlabach, theologian from the University of St. Thomas in Minnesota, USA. He and his wife Joetta Schlabach have opened their hands to publish this book of memory. I also appreciate their friends abroad who have helped with generous donations to accomplish this project. Although I do not know many of them personally, I say *lomlaj melti'oox*—thank you very much, in Tz'utujil.

I want to thank the bishops of Oklahoma, Sololá, and Chimaltenango, who have given moral and material support to our parish of Santiago Atitlán for so many decades. I also thank Cardinal Ramazzini, bishop of Huehuetenango, for the words of encouragement that open this book by acknowledging the same "voice" that Father Apla's also listened to.

The hope that we have shared from the beginning of this project is that it will especially help young Atitecos and Tz'utujiles to remember what has happened in our beloved town, and never, ever, forget. Therefore, it is necessary to thank the very people of Santiago Atitlán for their historic, firm, and peaceful struggle to achieve peace and defend human dignity, both here in our region and throughout the Guatemalan nation. May our young people continue in that struggle. May we all respect the human rights that God and his son Jesus Christ have granted us, desiring that we love one another as sisters and brothers, always saying no to violence.

Juan Ajtzip

Santiago Atitlán, Sololá, Guatemala

⁓

Together with Juan Ajtzip, I would like to thank a number of people who have offered support and encouragement as this project has developed. Father Germán Navarro and the late Deacon John Donaghy of the Santa Rosa de Copán diocese in northwestern Honduras are the two pilgrims whose dinner conversation in early 2018 was so providential in prompting the project (see pages xx–xxi). Father Kevin McDonough and Deacon Bill Heinen of the Sagrado Corazón de Jesús parish in South Minneapolis offered counsel and logistical support as I set up a small fundraising effort to defray expenses. Through the advocacy of my old friend Phil McManus, the Appleton Foundation of Santa Cruz, California, provided a seed money grant. Special thanks go to Father John Klassen OSB, former abbot of Saint John's Abbey (Minnesota), and to Father McDonough for their leadership donations.

Here in Guatemala, Deacon Nate Bacon has accompanied us with his seemingly endless enthusiasm, offered advice, and helped us make key connections. Among those connections, members of CONFREGUA, the Confederation of Religious in Guatemala, have welcomed this project warmly and are extending our network with a view toward promoting publication of the Spanish edition. We are especially honored and grateful to Cardinal Álvaro Ramazzini for his willingness to write such a kind and incisive foreword to this book.

In the Archdiocese of Oklahoma City, which has built a shrine and fine museum to honor Blessed Stanley Rother and to house his body and other relics, I received a kind welcome from Archbishop Paul Coakley and Deacon Norman Mejstrik when my wife and I visited in 2023. The archdiocesan archivist, George Rigazzi, opened the Rother archives as I searched for a photo that might show Padre Apla's and Juan Ajtzip together in the days of their collaboration in the 1970s. Though we came up short, Rigazzi's hospitality more than compensated. Also in Oklahoma City, María Ruiz Scaperlanda, Rother's biographer, welcomed this complement to her own work and offered good counsel when we met with her over coffee at a Starbucks near the archdiocesan offices.

Special thanks go to Olga Piedresanta in Guatemala City, who copyedited our Spanish manuscript, which was especially necessary, since Tz'utujil is Juan's native tongue and English is mine. My wife Joetta Handrich Schlabach also proofread the first draft of my English translation, which was especially necessary because I had lived with the Spanish text so long that Spanishisms were starting to seem natural. I am of course grateful to Joetta for her many other forms of support. She has accompanied me on so many Central American adventures over the years, and now on our annual migration to Santiago Atitlán. Living in Santiago would be nearly unimaginable, however, without the hospitality of Juan Ajtzip and his entire extended family, who have all but written adoption papers in order to make us feel at home. To honor them, Juan, his colleagues, and his friend Padre Apla's among the *najb'eey taq ri'jaa'*—the ancestors and elders—is itself a great honor.

Gerald W. Schlabach
Santiago Atitlán, Sololá, Guatemala,
and Grand Marais, Michigan, USA

# Introduction

*Gerald W. Schlabach*

Roman Catholics, the Eastern Orthodox, and other Christians for many reasons treasure memories of the holy ones in their traditions. We begin with the biblical affirmation of the Letter to the Hebrews 12:1, that those who persevere on the great pilgrimage of faith and discipleship are surrounded by a "great cloud of witnesses." Thus may we trust that we have very present, though unseen, companions. We are not alone, and indeed we may find encouragement both in their examples and in their intercessions. Simply to recount their histories is to take the first step in learning, then imitating, then growing in practices of virtue and holiness.

Down through the centuries, however, "the lives of the saints" have become a genre, with two opposite tendencies. One tendency is to accentuate the most exotic parts of the stories of the saints or to delight most in the more florid of characters in the canon of recognized saints. The opposite tendency, paradoxically, is to stylize but thus flatten out these lives, as though saintliness came in a standard format or formula. Among Catholics, standardized devotional practices then kick in. At best, this is a way to honor those whom the Vatican officially recognizes first as "servants of God," then as "venerable," then as "blessed," on the way to inclusion among the saints. But what can start to get lost with both tendencies is the actual humanity, the formative contexts, and the specific lessons of these lives.

This book seeks to prevent that from happening to Father Stanley Francis Rother—missionary priest from Oklahoma, pastor in Guatemala's Santiago Atitlán, affectionately named Padre Apla's by the Tz'utujil Maya he loved. Assassinated on 28 July 1981, he was recognized as a martyr by Pope Francis in 2016 and was named "Blessed" in 2017. But he is already a saint to those among whom he ministered and for whom he gave his life.

The fine biography of Rother by María Ruiz Scaperlanda, *The Shepherd Who Didn't Run*, is certainly not guilty of hagiography in a fabulizing sense. Indeed, it is indispensable for its retrieval of the concrete historical data of Rother's life. But Juan Ajtzip did not know of that book, which was not yet available in Spanish, when in January 2018, only a few months after Rother's beatification, he asked me to help him figure out how to write about Rother. And in any case, Scaperlanda could only begin to convey the full-bodied context that Ajtzip now offers. That offering is a firsthand account of Father Stanley's impact from a Maya perspective—a memory of Rother, embedded in a memoir of Juan's own life, embedded within the Atiteca community, as those who live in the region of Santiago Atitlán refer to themselves.

What's more, neither Ajtzip's memoir nor Rother's "life" should be abstracted from the brutally concrete context of Guatemala in the second half of the twentieth century. Until the year before Rother's martyrdom in 1981, the Santiago Atitlán region had largely avoided *la Violencia*—as Guatemalans refer to the repression by which the country's military government sought to quell any possibility that the majority-indigenous population would rise up to support a leftist guerrilla movement. That repression was prompted by military dictatorships first imposed through the coup that the United States manufactured in 1954. That coup snuffed out a reform-minded democratic government that, though inspired more by Franklin Roosevelt's "four freedoms" than by Marxism, thus became a casualty of Cold-War obsessions. Guatemala's ensuing civil war lasted more than 35 years. Of the estimated 250,000 lives lost in *la Violencia*, some 90 percent were killed either by the Guatemalan military or by paramilitary groups doing its clandestine bidding. This, according to exhaustively documented reports following Guatemala's 1996 Peace Accord, conducted both by a United Nations commission and by the Human Rights Office of the Archdiocese of Guatemala City. The overwhelming majority of those victims (83 percent) were indigenous people.[1]

1 The 90 percent figure is from REMHI, *Guatemala: Never Again!* Recovery of Historical Memory Project: Official Report, Human Rights Office, Archdiocese of Guatemala, foreword by Thomas Quigley (Maryknoll, NY: Orbis Books, 1999), 290. An even higher figure of 93 percent appears in the UN-commissioned report by the Commission for Historical Clarification, *Guatemala: Memory of Silence: Tz'inil Na'Tab'Al*, Conclusions and Recommendations, Report for the United Nations Office of Project Services (UN-OPS) (Guatemala: Academy of Mayan Languages of Guatemala, 1999), 33—available at https://hrdag.org/wp-content/uploads/2013/01/CEHreport-english.pdf. The figure of 83 percent indigenous victims appears in the latter, on p. 85.

Father Stanley Francis Rother sought assiduously to avoid political alliances and, as Juan Ajtzip's testimony confirms, he preached energetically and consistently against every resort to violence. Still, in the Guatemalan context of the 1970s and early 1980s, simply to accompany the indigenous Maya as a pastor, to defend their dignity from the pulpit, and to oppose human rights abuses against them, was to invite suspicion and eventually death threats. Once, when asked if he was involved politically, Father Stanley explained: "To shake the hand of an Indian is a political act."[2]

This reality was precisely the tragic bind that forced impossible choices in these decades onto so many Guatemalans and their international friends. Such was the case even when they sought to improve conditions among the poor through nonviolent means and mere reform, rather than armed revolution. The attempt by the military governments of Guatemala, and successive US administrations backing them, to quell support for insurgents through indiscriminate repression worked—when it *did* work— only through fear and terror and a trauma that lingers among Guatemalans to this day. Often, it did not work at all, for it simply convinced many conscientious activists that reformist strategies or nonviolent tactics were doomed to failure.

Both Juan Ajtzip and his mentor Padre Apla's continued placing their hope in development projects, nonviolent means, and patient reform, rather than violent revolution. But in fact, Guatemala's elites were deciding that even these were too threatening, too revolutionary. For if the indigenous and other impoverished Guatemalans could organize their own health projects and agricultural co-ops—and radio stations—what other force might they find in numbers and in solidarity? Part of the quiet drama of this book is that Juan Ajtzip was somehow savvy enough and lucky enough to thread the needle, survive, and live to share his memoir and his testimony of Rother. If others were either less lucky or felt forced into other decisions, perhaps the reader will better understand why.

Juan Ajtzip was the first Maya director of *La Voz de Atitlán*—The Voice of Atitlán—a radio station founded by the missionary team Micatokla that

2 María Ruiz Scaperlanda, *The Shepherd Who Didn't Run: Father Stanley Rother, Martyr from Oklahoma* (Huntington, IN: Our Sunday Visitor Publishing Division, 2015), 223.

arrived from Oklahoma in the 1960s. The radio station offered far more than entertainment. As chapter 5 explains, it served as the point of integration for many of the parish's efforts to more fully live out an integral or wholistic gospel message. Though Rother became its guide and Ajtzip its director, what matters most is the way it allowed many other *compañeros* or colleagues to coordinate all of their fresh initiatives to serve the common good. They did so not only on the radio, but through grassroots catechism, literacy work, and cooperatives, in towns all around the shore of Lake Atitlán. As Cardinal Ramazzini astutely points out in his foreword, the protagonists in this story are not just the author and the martyred priest, but the people of Santiago.

Ajtzip believes that he himself escaped kidnapping, torture, and death during the period of greatest repression, in which Rother died, only because an illness had forced him to take a leave of absence from the radio. During the time when Rother was supervising the repair of the church in Santiago, Ajtzip also served as secretary on the reconstruction committee. He was active both among parish catechists and as a member of Catholic Action, serving in leadership roles in both groups in the mid-1980s. The Guatemalan bishops invited Ajtzip to be part of the delegation to Oklahoma for Rother's beatification in September 2017.

A primary-school teacher as well as a community organizer, Ajtzip was instrumental in bringing schools both to new neighborhoods in Santiago and to a number of surrounding rural villages. He was a key source for anthropologists Robert Carlsen and Sandra Orellana, authors of two important books on the Tz'utujil Maya of Santiago, though for security reasons he asked them to keep his name out of their books. I first met Juan Ajtzip upon the recommendation of Monsignor Gregory Schaffer, another missionary priest for some 50 years in nearby San Lucas Tolimán. For almost 20 years I then relied on Ajtzip to orient students from the University of St. Thomas in Minnesota concerning Santiago's history.

Central America had been shaping my life since I first went there as a teenager in the 1970s, and Guatemala had been my greatest teacher. As I anticipated retiring from the classroom, though not from scholarship, I sensed that I owed a debt to its people, especially the Maya. When in early January 2018 I was sitting in a restaurant with a priest and a permanent deacon from Honduras who had made a pilgrimage together to the site of Rother's ministry, a turn in the conversation was a providential moment for both Juan Ajtzip and me. Juan's desire to tell the story of his relationship to Padre Apla's grew from two nagging concerns: (1) the steady erosion of the Maya culture, especially among young people, in the face of pressures from globalization, and (2) a continuing need among Catholics for Rother's social vision and openness to creative inculturation in the parish. Then as now, Juan Ajtzip's hope has been to encourage Tz'utujil Maya pride in their cultural identity, even as he encouraged fellow Catholics—now so grateful for the Church's recognition of the beloved pastor whose relics they guard—to continue living out the vision of Padre Apla's, not simply to honor him through their devotional practices.

A year later, I had read Scaperlanda's biography of Rother closely, along with other research, and convinced a reticent Juan that his own life story could provide invaluable background to Rother's ministry and impact. Having mulled over how to intertwine the two histories, I returned to Santiago and recorded some 20 hours of interviews with Ajtzip. Edited transcripts of those interviews eventually constituted the very rough first draft of this book.

If the final product now retains a few colloquialisms, redundancies, and slightly literal translations of indigenous phrasings from that origin in interviews, this may be fortuitous. After all, to speak of Padre Apla's and his impact in a Maya "voice" has been our foremost goal. To be sure, I have sometimes needed to press Juan to supply background information for a wider audience both in *ladina* (culturally nonindigenous) Guatemala and internationally. But in every other way, I as his editorial adviser have sought to preserve Juan's voice, both as a person and as a Maya community leader. His culture is an oral culture, and both as a teacher and as a radio broadcaster he is a master storyteller. So even as he asked my help in moving to keyboard and paper, I have welcomed a certain conversational quality that would convey his voice.

⁓

Inevitably, some readers may pause before at least two aspects of the account here. First, is the work of missionaries among indigenous peoples even legitimate? After all, the way that Christianity came to Latin America and elsewhere is inextricable from the history of violent colonialization. Second, have the development projects that Ajtzip, Micatokla, and Rother promoted actually brought some of the acids of globalization that Juan bemoans?

Ajtzip is certainly not blind to the injustices of the Spanish Conquest and its continuing legacy. In this regard, the reader will often find him quite blunt. However, as a loyal Catholic, who remains grateful for ways that the gospel of Jesus Christ has nonetheless been faithfully proclaimed and has shaped his own life, Juan is more diplomatic about the Catholic Church as he knows it in Guatemala. For one thing, he survived *la Violencia* in part by being constitutionally diplomatic, and I think he finds it hard to abandon that mode in any context now. But above all, in the work of Micatokla, especially in the culturally respectful pastoral practices of Blessed Stanley Rother, he saw the best of Catholic evangelization. If anything, these ministries can be seen as an effort to repent from and correct for earlier mistakes. They thus offer a template for pastors and missionaries today.

In any case, diplomatic as he is, between the lines Ajtzip does offer continuing criticisms of evangelizing and pastoral practices that violate or at least obscure the teachings of Jesus. Those who rightly critique colonialism and continuing neocolonialism for the damage they have done to indigenous cultures would do well to include a voice such as his among primary sources for their analysis. After all, a commitment to listening to those who have long been suppressed requires no less.

Ajtzip also offers a primary source for analyzing the complex dynamics of globalization and the prospects of cultural survival by peoples such as his. There are ways in which the "development" that he has promoted throughout his life and career, through both the mentorship of Blessed Stanley Rother and the example of his own forebears, may have contributed to the very globalization and cultural erosion that Juan laments. Accounts of the two dynamics appear here together, juxtaposed without any obvious reconciliation. If there is a paradox or a dilemma here—and surely there is—it is evident in much of human history in the last century or longer. We can hardly ask Juan Ajtzip to be more than a witness to this drama.

Blessed Father Stanley "Apla's" Rother dressed in a chasuble
embroidered with Maya motifs. (Courtesy of the Archives of the
Archdiocese of Oklahoma City.)

# CHAPTER 1

# The miracle of 1990

As the year 1990 was ending, the people of Santiago Atitlán were tired out in every way from all the abuses we had experienced since 1980. We *campesinos* lived from our work in the countryside, walking every day to the fields to cultivate our small plots of land. But when we went to the countryside, we encountered clashes between the guerrillas and the army, in addition to the dead, the corpses, the military patrols. We risked being the next to be accused of supporting the guerrillas and then being disappeared. Crops were lost, or people stopped farming altogether. Families went hungry, with no work in the fields. People speculated about the clashes: What was provoking them? Where did they come from?

The people longed for a real peace. We longed to find a peaceful way of living as families and working without being bothered. Blessed Father Stanley Francis Rother had preached to us that the true peace announced by the Gospel comes by loving and supporting one another as brothers and sisters. But the authorities were killing the catechists he had trained through Bible studies and who shared Jesus' message of peace. And in 1981 they had killed him.

There was no peace. It was a time of hatred and violence. Still, Padre Apla's—as we call him in our Mayan language of Tz'utujil—had not left us.

## THE PEOPLE UNITE

There came a time when some people who live in the Xechivoy neighborhood saw a bunch of people who were up to no good come into their neighborhood. The scoundrels had spent the night drinking and came to a house in the community to kidnap the father of a family, Andrés Sapalú Ajuchán. Some reports say that his attractive daughter had caught their attention.[1] Some young men were sitting in the street. They saw the intruders pass by and that they were armed. The young men were watching from down the street as the intruders went up to the Sapalú Ajuchán house. When the men entered the house, the family screamed. As the family shouted, the young men sitting in the street understood that they meant harm and might kidnap the family. They began to scream too.

The street there is a dead end, with no other way back, and quite a few young people were watching. They all converged, tried to grab the men, and ran after them when they tried to escape. They chased them and saw that eventually they entered the military base that was one kilometer outside the town of Santiago. At the entrance, they tried to explain to the soldiers who were guarding the base that they had chased men who were harassing a family. When the guards did not listen, the young men decided to warn the town authorities, both the outgoing mayor and the recently elected incoming mayor, who was about to take office. They also alerted the *cabecera* of the town, the communal leader of the Tz'utujiles. The idea was to call the entire population together and see if all the community leaders were willing to accompany them.

At that point, the young men split up, since there were a lot of them. One group stayed on watch, and another group went to warn the town authorities. It was twelve o'clock at night, but they started waking up the town. People were saying, "It's the army that is killing us!" They started ringing the church bell. They were preparing to go ask why the soldiers were there and to get the intruders out of the military base. They were going to speak to the head of the base.

Soon the whole town—thousands of people—went to the military base to demand an explanation. To communicate their nonviolent intent, many carried white flags. But it didn't go well. The military officers did not listen. They did not want a serious dialogue with the civilian authorities. They answered us badly. In fact, they answered us with guns and killed 13 people, including a boy who had been a student of mine, Jerónimo Sojuel

1. Jorge Murga Armas discusses the various versions of the incident without reaching a conclusion as to which is true. See Jorge Murga Armas, *Santiago Atitlán: organización comunitaria y seguridad de los habitantes*, in Spanish and Tz'utujil, Programa Sistema Penal y Derechos Humanos, ILANUD / European Commission, Tz'utujil translation by Juan Vásquez Tuiz (Guatemala: Cholsamaj, 1997), 2022.

Sisay. Approximately 40 people were also left wounded. Those 13 dead were left lying in the coffee fields in front of the base. The crowd shouted, "Get down!," and many ran through the coffee trees, hiding behind the stones until dawn and crying loudly.

With this spontaneous organization, the people united. A banner was hung in front of the Catholic church that read "Army of assassins out of Santiago Atitlán." The mayors and the *cabecera* of the town joined with a group of other people. They asked various organizations such as the directors of the radio station, *La Voz de Atitlán*, to choose representatives of the people to go before the central government. They organized themselves, formed a committee, and that committee began to work. The committee, the people, and the local authorities agreed to join with human rights organizations to complain to the government. They contacted journalists and activists, inside the country and even abroad. They did not allow anyone to move the corpses until journalists could arrive to take pictures and document the truth of the events. They also did not allow stores to sell food and fuel to the soldiers, so that they had to buy from other villages around Lake Atitlán and bring supplies in by boat.

The next day after the massacre, there was another march, where many organizations from other parts of Guatemala showed solidarity with our demand to live in peace. Journalists came in the morning to take pictures, which were soon published in the national and international press. I think that news of the massacre even reached the United States. The next day the question was ringing through the press and on television: "What is happening in Santiago?"

The committees that had organized asked the people themselves to come together to watch over one another in their own neighborhoods. The committees that the people had appointed and the local authorities agreed that the people themselves should monitor their own people. Based on this agreement, we traveled a few days later to human rights offices in the capital to meet with the national authorities.

The president at that time was Vinicio Cerezo of the Christian Democracy party. His administration was a little more open than some others, both before and after. After two or three days, they accepted our proposal. And a few days later the authorities came to sign a document, an official act of government. According to this act, the town would remain totally without a military base. In fact, nobody was to touch any weapons. No one.

It was forbidden here, be it on one side or the other. No one was allowed to bear arms. The people themselves guaranteed their own security.

To do this, we took a roll in each neighborhood and formed our own unarmed patrols. There were inspections of cars entering town, at the docks where boats arrived—everywhere. Neighborhood committees patrolled both night and day. We watched things very closely. That was the agreement we reached, first among ourselves and then with the national government, in order to achieve total peace in Santiago. That is how it worked out. The government removed the base, the military left, and the people were left to take care of the town themselves. After 30 years of civil war in Guatemala, we had achieved the first demilitarized zone in the whole country.[2]

## PADRE APLA'S, STILL WITH US

The massacre of those 13 people by the military, outside the base where the people confronted them, took place on December 2, 1990. From the next month onwards, Catholic Action and the parish priest of the Catholic church made plans to celebrate mass at the same place on the second of every month, in the name of the deceased. At each mass, the people remembered Blessed Father Stanley Francis Rother—Padre Apla's.

By remembering those events of 1990, after all, the people of Santiago Atitlán pay respect and honor to Father Stanley, who had died in the name of Jesus Christ some nine years before, but also in the name of the people of Santiago. He struggled and died so that there would be no violence in our town, preaching in the name of Jesus Christ. He lived among us for about 13 years, and we never heard him speak in favor of violence. For that reason, we feel that Father interceded for peace for our people when he came into the full presence of our heavenly Father. We felt his presence in this movement to achieve true peace for the good of our own lives.

When Padre Apla's was assassinated, his remains were taken to his homeland of Oklahoma in the United States, but the Atiteco people asked that his heart remain here, because he had given himself in love to his people of Santiago Atitlán. Some of his blood was sealed into a memorial

2. Histories of the 1990 nonviolent uprising appear in Morna Macleod, *Santiago Atitlán, ombligo del universo Tz'utujil: cosmovisión y ciudadanía* (Guatemala City: NOVIB, 2000), 15–22; and Donna Whitson Brett and Edward T. Brett, "The Tz'utujil Revolt," chapter 2 in *Martyrs of Hope: Seven U.S. Missioners in Central America* (Maryknoll, NY: Orbis Books, 2018), 35–42. Like Juan Ajtzip, authors Brett and Brett see a direct link between the ministry of Blessed Stanley Rother and the events of December 1990.

near the entrance of the church, and later the bishops and priests decided to put a vial of his blood under the altar where the Eucharist of the Holy Mass is celebrated. He remains among us, therefore. He is with us, accompanying his people always. Thus he accompanied the people out of their crisis, which had resulted from the deteriorating political crisis.

And the situation did not stop there. Thank God that due to all we had experienced, over time the people began to work hard again. We worked in the way that Padre Apla's and his companions had inspired us to do in the years before his assassination. The people began to work and look for ways to cooperate with each other, helping one another. With support from some national and Central American organizations, we started to train people again in the jobs they needed, for example, in tailoring, weaving, carpentry, baking, women in sewing, young people in painting and sculpture. And we started to offer the same possibilities to other neighboring municipalities as well.

When we have the support of all those people, we are able to work very well here in Santiago, helping the population, always with the support that the parish has given. To be able to work cooperatively in this way was one of the fruits of the 1990 peace agreement. Of course, like any town, we are always going to have robberies, assaults, and fights. But now, thank God, we have not had major problems like before—only the kind of problems that can happen in any town. We have been able to solve the minor problems we have had through our own local organizations, others who are in solidarity with us, and the local authorities, both civil and ecclesiastical.

The sad thing is that as the years have passed, the people's unarmed civil patrols have died out. Those who were there in the beginning got involved in politics, and so the committee was abandoned. But the people are always vigilant. The people are always ready with their whistles. When a problem develops, people take out their whistles and start shouting. Even though we no longer have organized patrols making rounds, the people are ready for anything. We hope the youth will maintain the same enthusiasm.

## IT WAS A MIRACLE

Father Stanley loved this town very much. He wanted the people to live in peace, without hatred, without theft, without murder. His wish was that we hear what the word of God tells us in the Gospels—that we love one another, and that we also forgive one another many times. His desire was

5

that the elders would live well together with their children. He loved the people so much. Yes, and he is still with us with that love. So really, for me, what he has done for our people is a miracle.

Blessed Father Stanley "Apla's" Rother. (Photo by Father David Monahan, courtesy of the Archives of the Archdiocese of Oklahoma City.)

After all, almost ten years after Father Stanley's death, this breakthrough of peace and tranquility came to the town. It came because he is in heaven, interceding to God for us. His prayers join together with our own prayers and those of our brothers and sisters who have worked for the good of the people—old men and old women, boys and girls, all through the years. He is truly with his people.

I am convinced that he has given us total support for the miracle that the people received from God through him, to mobilize together to achieve peace and tranquility. It was truly a miracle that the authorities accepted the peace accords. That's how I know that God is with us. I thank God for the presence of Father Stanley, who lived in Santiago Atitlán and asked God for this miracle from heaven for the people of Santiago. He listened to us when he lived with us as a pastor, accompanying our people, and he continues to listen to us now.

There are others also who have dedicated their energy here in Santiago, some giving their lives, some dying as well. They must be praying for us too, asking God to take care of us. We should thank the people who have given their lives in Santiago for those miracles that took place in Santiago Atitlán, by working together for peace, harmony, and dialogue.

It was through dialogue—not through arms or fighting—that we won this peace. When the people rose up peacefully to protest against military abuses, many people of different faiths in Santiago Atitlán demonstrated total unity. They were Evangelicals and Catholics. There were elders, children, all together in one voice and in one love for God. There were Maya spiritual practitioners from the *cofradías*. All those who have died together with Padre Apla's have given us a miracle of love, of strength, to ask and to be able to talk to the people.

In those days we even managed to talk to the president of Guatemala, and he recognized the people's need. As I recall, the president told us something like this: "I agree! It is not me, by means of a signature on a piece of paper, who has achieved this. It is thanks to all those who worked to achieve these dialogues. And I am very grateful. And I hope in God that future young people will work together for good—that they will use these great ideas that can serve us in the future to do good through dialogue. I hope that in this way many necessities of life will be achieved, in service to the children, the elderly, the people in need." So, yes, if peace was achieved, it is because of the blood of our brothers and sisters who have given themselves in our town.

That is why for so many years mass was celebrated on the second of every month, at the place where the 13 people died. I thank God that, through the parish, the priests continued to celebrate the mass for many years, and the people participated. Now it is every year that they celebrate, and many people come, remembering. We keep the memory alive by doing this every year. We hope not to forget what happened.

But this also means that we learned a lesson: Let's not fall back into violence and repression. The people want peace, tranquility. That is why Father Thomas McSherry, the pastor who came after Father Stanley was martyred, built the Peace Park, a beautiful park on the same site as the massacre. The names of each of the 13 people who lost their lives were written on crosses there. Father Thomas wanted us to remember our peace, and our people. The park leaves us a good example, reminding us to live peacefully, without people carrying weapons to take the lives of others. Who has the power to end the lives of others? No one. Only God. God has given the gift of life. We are very grateful. We must work, work for the good of all.

# CHAPTER 2

# Life in Santiago Atitlán

LIFE IN THE TIME of my childhood was hardly childhood in today's sense. As children of the Maya Tz'utujil people of Santiago Atitlán, we did not enjoy any of the rights we needed to grow and thrive. Our lives and those of children in many parts of Guatemala could sometimes be painful.

First of all, there was not enough food for a family. There were not enough jobs for the parents, or they were not paid well when they had jobs. So parents didn't have enough to support a family. There was very little clothing. We didn't have electric lights in our homes, or on the streets. We didn't have mechanized mills for our corn. We had no clean drinking water. All the families used the lake, both for washing clothes and for family use. There were endless problems—lots of diseases, measles, whooping cough. Many, many children died.

## CHILDHOOD

I had a hard childhood, with very little opportunity for recreation. As children we had to accompany our parents to work in the fields, doing whatever we could do. The good thing is that we learned to work, with respect for our elders and our culture, something that does not always happen today. But if you wanted to play at night as a child, you couldn't, because there were no lights. It was dark in all the streets! We had to go into the house early with the family. Nobody walked on the street after seven or eight o'clock at night. Everybody was asleep.

Recreation was almost nonexistent for us. Of course, as children we always played some games in the street, during the day or in the evenings after chores, at five or six o'clock. Sometimes we went out to the churchyard or played in the municipal park. But it was never for very long. We had to go out to work at six in the morning, after all. We had to walk two to three hours to get to the field to plant. It was a lot—up the hills and then down. We would arrive at 8:30 or 9:00 to work. Then we drank a little water and ate a tortilla with salt, or maybe without salt. We would stay until 3:00 in the afternoon, leaving to return to town—another two-to-three-hour walk. Then at 5:00 or 5:30 we got home for the family meal. That took another 30 to 40 minutes to eat. By the time we finished it was 6:00, and already it was getting dark.

We couldn't throw any tantrums, or get into any mischief as children, because our parents always grabbed us to punish us. Some parents put us to work instead of hitting us. They might not be violent, but if we made mistakes, they gave us extra work at home. Sundays were cleaning days. Clean up the street, clean up our place, so you couldn't see any garbage on the street. Nothing. If we dropped a kernel of corn, "Pick it up," they said. If we didn't pick it up, then they would pull our ears—that's a discipline our parents used to do.

Of course, other family disciplines were very nice. Mothers spent their days embroidering and weaving clothes for the whole family. No one dressed like outsiders. When we arrived from the field, our mother began to make food from what we had brought—*chipilín* and other edible herbs. This gave us a little chance to play for a while before the meal. Then our father would say, "Well, come and eat, everybody now." There was no table or anything like that, but we did form a circle. In other words, our mother would make a little circle and give us big tortillas—very thin, very nice. And sometimes we had also brought little fish, because the people with land on the shore of the lake caught little fish. We had a little piece of land from my mother's side of the family on the shore of the lake, and loaned to some fishermen, so they sometimes gave us a basket of fish in exchange. Our mother would then cook the fish for dinner. We all ate together as a family. (Nowadays the customs have changed in some families. Everyone starts eating when they are hungry.)

Despite the harshness of life, there were certain benefits. We were able to have a little fun on holidays, though at the time that meant only the town's annual festival. There was marimba, our typical marimba, but no saxophones, no horns. Just marimbas, like the Mayeey group has. People danced and drank their *cuxa*, the typical guaro of the town. But that was about all, just the town festival on the feast of St. James the Apostle on July 25. The *cofradías* do celebrate other events—Lent, the Holy Week processions, and the major days of worship from Palm Saturday to Easter. But other holidays, like All Souls' Day, Christmas, New Year's Day—people celebrated the end of the year without fireworks or lights. It was never a big party, like now, because there wasn't much money.

I completed only three grades of elementary school. Because of the need for labor, our parents could not send us to a junior high or high school. Besides, school was another expense back then. There was only one official Spanish language school with first through fourth grade. Although it was public, there were always expenses like clothing, food, and supplies, plus the loss of six hours of daily labor for the family. We did not have private schools either. There were many children and few teachers. It was not easy to go to school when parents needed our help to make ends meet.

## HARD WORK

That is why, when I was only twelve years old, I started to accompany my older brothers and father to the coast, to work some months of the year. When I say the coast, I'm talking about places in the south—Suchitepéquez, the Tiquisate area, Chipo and other plantations, San Marcos, Sololá—that whole area of the coast. They harvest twice as much there as in mountainous areas. I worked there for about five years when I was young. I worked on the plantations, picking cotton and coffee and cutting sugar cane.

We never worked on our own land there. On the coast we worked for others. When you rent land, you have to pay rent to plant hay, or to take care of the cattle, or to plant a fruit tree. But after two or three years, the farmer has to leave the land after having cleaned it and worked it up. So even when we planted our own corn or grazed cattle, we still had to go and work on other farms. That is what made life so hard.[1]

1. According to many analysts, the agrarian land tenure system that has been imposed over the last two centuries is the predominant factor in Guatemalan politics. Modern development has displaced the indigenous communal property system with the private property system, and production has become increasingly export-oriented. Using various economic, quasi-legal, and sometimes violent means, major landowners, whether national or international companies, have become owners of the best land, especially on the West coast, while indigenous and poor ladinos have been left with mountainous

If we worked on land here in Atitlán, it was by renting land from other people. But there was not much produce here in the highlands either. There were some products—avocados for example—but nobody bought them. There was a harvest, but much got thrown away and lost. No one grew coffee yet. Some people grew a few vegetables on the shore of the lake, tomatoes and chili peppers more than anything else. Some grew peaches. My father rented land, but it was very expensive to irrigate the tomatoes. Besides, the land here is very sandy and rocky. So we harvested crops only once a year. In contrast, on the coast, farmers get two harvests a year. People went there if they could get land, because it was more productive, and we needed corn. Because that is what we live on. The people from Tecpán, to the north of us, sold produce, but it was very expensive; without work, we couldn't afford it. So we had to plant our own corn and try to be self-sufficient.

Our mothers also worked a lot. It was very hard work for the women, the mothers of the family. They had to go to bring water from the lake and carry a jar of water and also clean clothes—washing our clothes on the shore of the lake. It was a huge burden for them, going down to the lake and back. We lived up the hill, which meant they had a lot to carry. They didn't have anything mechanized, so they had to kneel at a stone to grind corn. They began by soaking corn overnight in lye water, then grinding the corn into *masa* to make tortillas. There were no machines; it was hard work!

To sum up, we young people did not enjoy recreation and other activities together as we really should. No. There was no time to waste. Our parents wouldn't give us any vacation, even for a day or two. Sundays we went to work and then to mass. It was a break for parents just to give their children three or four hours off every Sunday.

It was because of these conditions that we young people went to pick cotton—"walking the line," we called it—in the municipality of La Concepción, Escuintla. We learned the work, but it was a very hard life. Despite the need to go to the coast for a few months each year to get work, it was very risky. Life on the coast was even harder than here, because there was a lot of malaria. I got sick from that, as many young people did.

---

land divided into small plots. This has guaranteed the large landowners an impoverished population in need of seasonal labor willing to work for low pay—although sometimes they had to forcibly recruit as well. In these paragraphs, Juan is indicating that in his youth, he had to participate in this system. In chapter 6 he talks more about the system, which is called *latifundismo*. For more information and analysis regarding this system, see Thomas and Marjorie Melville, *Guatemala: The Politics of Land Ownership* (New York: The Free Press, 1971).

I was born here, and I think I'm going to die here. I've worked in a few other places, mostly on the coast. I was also in Nahualá for a year to learn broadcasting and radio administration. I visited their villages and towns, supervising schools for radio broadcasting. I really enjoyed getting to know more about people's lives, and still do. That's how I have been able to learn something of the life of the people—from the coastal heat to the mountain cold in villages to the west of our country. This is how I have learned to live among the people.

## SEEKING A LIFE WITH DIGNITY

After a few years, I wanted to improve my life. I learned to weave typical fabrics on large looms. At that time, women wove on small backstrap looms, while men learned to weave, but on large wooden looms, with a shuttle. I also learned to work on sewing machines. My father had told me many times that we had to work, and we had to look for a job to be able to support our family. As I have already explained, we always accompanied our parents to work here in Santiago, planting various kinds of vegetables. With the little we had, we planted and worked together.

My father never gave up. He had been a soldier for seven years in the barracks, because he was very young when his parents died, and he was orphaned. The army grabbed him and took him to the barracks. When he got out, he was ready to work hard. He didn't want to look for work as an employee of the rich or with landowners. He didn't want to work for those people at all. He made his own way. He started working, selling beans and tomatoes—products from here in Santiago. If he could make a penny more in profit, he would travel to the coast. He went on foot with some *cacastes*, or wooden frames with agave rope, which is used for carrying loads. This is how our ancestors traveled as far as Chicacao or San Antonio Suchitepéquez and on to Mazatenango. Then, turning around, they would buy bananas there to bring here or take them to Tecpán. To travel to Tecpán, they had to go first by canoe, rowing, rowing, rowing, until they reached San Antonio Palopó. From there they would walk on foot again up to Tecpán. A lot, a lot, a lot of work. And then they would return with lime or corn to bring back here, because there wasn't enough corn here.

So life was hard in those days. My father earned a little more than what other *campesinos* earned here, by working with other people. Even so, the work was poorly paid. For my dad, the biggest advantage was that, although the work was always hard, it was his own. We had to work in some way or another to support the family. Not everybody was going to do what he did, because it was very demanding to hike like that. Carrying those kinds of loads was exhausting work. He worked like that with a group of eight or ten men. They would go together on foot, walking there and returning, carrying another canoe. They were together, because our custom is that we work together.

All those things were exhausting. But that's what life has dealt us here. We could not expect support from the authorities in our town. There was none because the municipalities did not receive any portion of the national budget. Nor did we have much connection with the national economy. No one could have imagined buying bottled water or having so many brands to choose from, as we do now. Nothing like that existed then. There was no plastic, not even a little bit. There was no nylon. Shoes? Either there were none, or they were very hard and uncomfortable. We only had locally made *caites* (leather sandals worn by the Maya and other *campesinos*).

It was like that even with the food. Nowadays food vendors fill the streets. But not back then. You couldn't buy food outside the house. There was nothing of the sort. You had to prepare your own food. We depended on poultry, chicks, and eggs. You had to raise chickens to eat an egg. The only commerce was between neighbors—at first only through barter. I saw bartering, and I lived it too. For example, you have corn and I have beans. We each exchange a pound, right? That's the way people used to do things. There was no need for someone to have a lot of money in order to buy. Many years ago, in fact, exchange happened by way of cacao; cacao was used for currency. That was before my time, but yes, I saw bartering. It was still going on. That was the way people used to work.

Another thing: our houses were small and made of straw, cane, and stone. That's how we lived. I remember once—I think it was in the 1940s—that a house burned down in the Panúl neighborhood nearby and set fire to hundreds of other houses, because they were all made of straw. The houses were close, and there was very strong wind. So many people were left even poorer than before! This is our history.

People also suffered because there was no health center at the time. There was no medical attention. As I recall, there was only one nurse in town. She would give you a penicillin injection for 25 cents. I once got sick, and the lady was too mean to give me medicine. A lot of people were dying from the diseases of the time—young people, old people, and children.

There were no vaccinations either—nothing like that. For me it was a very hard thing. I don't know how we made it. I don't know how we are still alive.

The good thing is that people used to know how to use medicinal herbs. When children got sick, they gave them their medicine. Sometimes it helped, sometimes it didn't, depending on who gave the medicine. There were people who knew how to cure with medicinal herbs. That was the only way we had to take care of ourselves. I remember one time when we all had whooping cough. Our parents gave us candy that they had soaked in kerosene. They left the candy to soak in the liquid for three or four hours. After that we put it in our mouths to eat. It was the only way we got relief from the cough.

## WHILE THE POLITICIANS CROON

The years of my childhood were very important for the nation of Guatemala, but I did not realize it. In the year 1944 a measure of democracy had arrived, as I have read. In 1952 the government attempted an agrarian reform, but it provoked a coup d'état sponsored by the United States in 1954. Here in Santiago we were touched very little by these political events. For many years it was like that. Everything that the political class promises in the city and in the departments remains in words. They say that there is a democracy, that there are agreements, that the congress has approved some laws. They croon about a lot of things, but things stay the same. As for what goes directly to the rural towns where people are suffering: nothing!

In the times before I was born, there was no road to Santiago. No road of any kind, only trails. The first car, van, or truck had not yet come in. There was nothing like today's pickup trucks. I remember well, when I was about nine or ten years old and the first trucks came into Santiago Atitlán, a pickup truck and another truck. One came from the neighboring town of San Lucas Tolimán on the other side of the lake, and it was such a big event that all the people ran to go see. It must have been around 1956. Until then, there was nothing! While the politicians continued to croon in the city, the towns remained poor.

A few of us young people had certain prospects for enjoying the potential of youth. Our parents educated us in a hardworking way, as they could not send us to a school to study. However, there were ways to study in the afternoons and evenings in some programs. This is how my youth started to open up. For example, a group of young people started coming

14

together in the Catholic church. When North Americans began arriving in town and our parish got new priests, that is when I felt a hand reaching out. We young people began to participate in recreational activities that they brought—sports, libraries, social groups. I remember well when we started playing volleyball and soccer. We also learned about church teaching.

Getting involved in these activities, as well as learning trades like weaving, I began to make a living. I told my father that I no longer wanted to return to the coast, because the work there was too hard. I'm glad that my dad fought for me to learn new skills, because not all the youth in town had the same chance to learn. Many continued to leave to look for work.

## THE RICHNESS OF COMMUNAL LIFE

In spite of our suffering, we undoubtedly experienced many riches through communal life (*convivencia*[2]) and mutual help. Something that I remember very clearly, and that impressed me very much when I was younger, is the joy I felt living together with the people. It is something that I will never forget, to live together (*convivir*) with the people where one lives. Ever since I was young, I saw and sensed and worked for people to help each other. The person who did not have a house could build a house together with other people. Through the collaboration of many, a house could be built every Sunday. Some brought straw. Others brought twine. Others brought sticks. Others brought stones. Others already had a door and walls made of cane. Every Sunday they were able to build a house by helping the people. They didn't have to import materials from somewhere else. In those days we didn't know about sheet metal. The roof was made of straw. The walls were made of cane. It was all well made, and all from local materials.

It was a very rich life together. The women participated as well, making the food, making *atol* for refreshment. We call it *maatz'*, a natural drink made from corn. We also cultivated in common; we sowed corn, moving from one family's crops to another's, each in turn. We used to exchange seeds for cultivation. Collaboration was not obligatory, but it was our custom. How nice it is to live that way—smiling, working, talking, sharing. It's a very nice way of life. There is a great richness among us, with our traditional customs. That's what life was like for the Maya people before.

---

2. See glossary for a full explanation of the theological and cultural meaning of the words *convivencia* and *convivir*.

## ORGANIZING

The arrival of the North American missionaries had an impact on the whole community, but especially on us young people. It made for a total change from what was there before. Before, priests arrived only to say mass. I had participated as an acolyte in the church previously. But the Spanish priests didn't have much time to attend to the people. They would come to Santiago for a few hours, and then move on to other towns celebrating mass, serving three or four towns, until they reached Sololá.

With the arrival of Micatokla—the Catholic Mission of Oklahoma in the United States—we started to receive much more support. Micatokla came in 1964 or so. Father Ramón Carlín, Father Robert O'Brien, and Father Thomas Stanford were the first to arrive. Then Father Stanley came a few years later. That is where our collaboration began.[3] They started to get us organized, helping us find new ways to improve. They organized handicrafts with the participation of young people, for example. At the beginning, not many young people came. Either they didn't like it, or in some cases the parents didn't want their children to leave the house. At first, about 20 to 30 men participated. Later, women also participated. Handicraft, savings-and-credit, and agricultural cooperatives were formed. Everyone who wanted to be included was included, women and men.

When the North Americans arrived, they were able to dedicate themselves to the community more than the previous itinerant priests. This allowed them to emphasize the participation of the youth. They organized several activities and invited us to choose the ones that interested us the most. Many of us were in a catechetical group, and we liked it because there were talks in the church. From there, they offered to train us in a literacy project. They saw that the great majority of the people did not know how to read. Because they were illiterate, their work opportunities were limited, and they suffered many illnesses. In addition, illiterate people did not have the resources to understand the root causes of their problems. Micatokla gave us the opportunity to be literacy teachers—to work and help the people.

We were not paid to do this work. That was not the idea, but rather that we would collaborate with the youth, with the elderly, and with all the

3. In 1962, Pope John XXIII had asked the Catholic churches in the United States to show solidarity with the Latin American Catholic churches through direct collaboration between dioceses by sending missionaries. Micatokla was the response of the Diocese of Oklahoma City and Tulsa.

people who wanted to learn to read and write. To get us started, they invited us to meet every Sunday with a teacher who would help us finish our elementary school. What that teacher taught us on Sundays, we then had to take and do the same work with other people on Mondays, Tuesdays, and Wednesdays—three times a week. In other words, we shared in learning with the people. I already knew how to read and write. But the brilliance of the whole strategy was that the people would help one another, mutually.

I got into this literacy work when I was only 16 or 17, still young. Already I could feel how working together with other people was a help to them. This also motivated me to start studying at night. Doing the work that I could, I wanted to see what grade level I could reach. I wanted to go beyond the third grade, which is what I had achieved so far. I knew that advancing would give me more prospects. That's why I dedicated myself to more education. It was a struggle; it took a long time to reach the sixth grade. But eventually I got my basic education, and then I became a teacher, with the preschool children.

I was already thinking of getting married when I was 17 or 18 years old. I would have to admit that when you marry young, you can't anticipate very well what will come. I had the crazy idea that just because I had learned the trade of weaving and was starting to earn money, I could get a wife. So I fell in love with a young lady and got married. With time we began to form a family. My children were born. That is where I faced the challenge of seeing how we could improve our lives. I have five living children; another died as a youth—Esteban. I joke that I can't even count my grandchildren anymore. Actually, I have nine grandchildren and three great-grandchildren. Now I can say that I've grown up, but it's been quite a struggle!

# CHAPTER 3

# "The smell of the sheep"

THAT WAS OUR LIFE when I was young. Lacking land of our own in our communities, we needed to seek seasonal employment on the plantations, despite the low wages offered by the landowners. Going to the coast, riding in the trucks, cutting cotton, bananas, and coffee, I suffered. But I believe that God felt the pain of his people. With the arrival of the priests in our town, a new hope appeared.

## THE ARRIVAL OF MICATOKLA

The team from the Catholic Mission of Oklahoma, or Micatokla, arrived in 1964 with a strong emphasis on integral, wholistic evangelization. The team of missionaries included priests, nuns, and lay people. Their first priority was companionship with the people and the celebration of mass. In this way they identified themselves with the people. Soon they were discovering the needs in the community and began to work in all that concerns us as human beings, social and economic as well as spiritual. The people enthusiastically received them.

The missionaries introduced themselves, came to mass, and then in meetings began to accompany (*convivir con*) the people, both culturally and religiously. They interacted with young people socially. With this friendliness they identified with the people, as they began to organize the catechetical work, for example. They presented catechesis to us as a vocation, to evangelize on behalf of the people and with responsibility to help our own people by practicing the word of God through mutual aid.

Before Micatokla's arrival, there were no staff at all in the parish. Only a few catechists and elderly women were present, plus the lay organization Catholic Action, the Pro-Reconstruction Committee for the church, and the *cofrades*. Catholic Action began more or less in the 1940s. In those years Catholic Action did not yet promote social action activities, but only religious activities—visits with the sick in homes, consolations, burying the dead, prayers in church, preparation for marriage, first communions, and confirmations. A group called the Daughters of Mary had organized some activities for women and young ladies. But there was no program for young people. The parish program was only baptisms and first communions, and only now and then, because there were no resident priests. Priests came once a week at the most, because they were also attending other communities, in other towns. There simply were not enough priests. And those who came were not Guatemalans but Spanish Franciscans.

When the North American priests arrived as a team, it was easier for them to work and help the community. For example, they quickly became aware of the death rate among children. Many, many children were dying from measles and whooping cough, sometimes 10 to 15 children a day. Because of the malnutrition, it was very hard. The team set up a health center and started vaccinating the children. At first people didn't want to accept this, because they didn't know what vaccines were. But some who understood did accept and began to vaccinate their children, as well as the elderly, against these illnesses. To combat malnutrition among children and the elderly, they set up a nutrition program that gave a glass of milk every morning to anyone who wanted it, at no cost. With the collaboration of the *cofradías*, they authorized the use of a chapel across from the church that the *cofradías* controlled during Holy Week.

To confront the health issue, Micatokla brought nurses and specialists. They analyzed community needs and planned a clinic with a laboratory to test for diseases and do X-rays. They even began to plan for a hospital, someday. In education and in the radio station's literacy project, however, they immediately sought to employ and train us Tz'utujil. They began to organize an association with social activities for the welfare of the people, with special attention to those who lived along the lakeshore. The philosophy was this: they saw needs and tried to respond according to those needs, but always with the goal of educating the Atitecos, as people in the region of Santiago Atitlán call ourselves.

The mission team brought people to work in handicrafts. I remember a nun named Roberta who came as a missionary, but with the purpose of training young people in handicrafts. She was especially good at sculpture. She also worked on drawings and other media, teaching the new artisans so that they could sell their products to tourists who come to visit our town. Then they set up a little shop in front of the church. Of course, it was not enough to alleviate the economic conditions, but it was a beginning.

Micatokla also brought in one or two agronomists, to work with the farmers through cooperatives. They began to teach organic fertilizers and new methods of fishing. They even brought in a priest who worked as an advisor to the cooperative, Father Thomas Stafford. He was very personable. After all that, they worked on the construction of houses for widows.

Finally, they helped with education. They opened an educational center for children, a Montessori preschool, a small school that operated in the hall of the Xocomil Agricultural Cooperative. Micatokla helped young people to study both primary and basic education (it was called the Basic Education Institute of Santiago Atitlán) until they formalized a school. Then they helped a few young people to pursue careers in high school and university. Only a few young people participated, because in those days almost no one traveled outside of town to study. After a while, they also began to help send young men to the seminaries. Many went to the seminary, although not all of them followed priestly careers. The mission sent some of the youth out of town to improve themselves, in the hope that they would return to serve the people with their abilities.

## COLLABORATION WITH THE PEOPLE

Perhaps it was inevitable that the Micatokla team started with donations from the outside, but they soon began to look for more collaborative strategies. It was difficult to get people to participate all at once, because people were scared of new things. They had already known about a nutrition program in the 1960s from the Alliance for Progress that gave out bags of powdered milk. The initial reaction of the people had been, "We won't drink the milk because maybe it will do us harm or keep us from giving birth to children. Or maybe they will take our children away from us." In other words, outside programs were always suspect.

The Micatokla team gave out donations as well. At the beginning, there was no other option. They gave handouts because people had nothing to collaborate with. I observed this even in handicrafts, in cooperatives, in organizations, and in education. For example, how were people to send a child to school? Without donations, they couldn't. The same was true with literacy and other types of bilingual education. The radio station was organized for educational purposes. The mission wanted to work through radio as a means to take education out into the community, to extend the literacy project. The literacy strategy was never to have foreigners do everything. The North Americans did not go to the houses themselves, but organized people to help their own people. For radio equipment, of course, they had to import the technology as a donation. But overall, the best strategy was to involve the people in a collaborative way.

The same strategy was used in other projects, including construction. People collaborated in making their own houses, coming to meetings, and participating with their labor. In the youth programs, young people themselves collaborated to develop and promote soccer—something we had rarely had before. They organized recreational activities among themselves for both women and men.

Thanks to this commitment to collaboration with the Maya people of Santiago Atitlán, an association was founded in 1966 so that the community could manage the radio station itself. That association continues to this day, with bilingual popular education programs in both Spanish and Tz'utujil.

Even in the catechesis program, the priests sought collaboration with the lay people. The mission trusted that the people themselves could participate in evangelization and serve one another. This has helped animate the community. The Gospel finds expression because God asks us to help each other. It is the work of the people. The philosophy of the Micatokla missionaries from the beginning was to ask for the people's collaboration in carrying out the Gospel message.

## FATHER STANLEY

Father Stanley Francis Rother—Father Stanley in English, or Padre Apla's, as we affectionately call him, using the Tz'utujil version of his middle name—joined the Micatokla team in its fourth year here. He was a very good, even-tempered priest, and it was in his character to work closely and energetically with the people. He certainly bore the gift of evangelization from a very deep place inside him. In his soul he brought peace. God had taught him what it means to love one's neighbor, and the people felt it. More than any other priest, he discovered how to enter deeply into the culture of the people. He loved them. He understood the people as they were. This approach was evident, for example, in his relationship with the *cofradías* and the elders of the people.

I recall getting to know Father Stanley soon after he arrived. Of course, he was present at religious activities, especially mass. At that time, I was one of the watchmen of the parish, keeping watch three nights a week. My companion was don Diego Coché. Our shift was from six in the evening until six in the morning of the following day, when others took over. We greeted Father when he arrived. He was a new priest, and we talked with him. He did not know Spanish very well yet, although later he learned a lot. But he understood us and said, "How are you?," and greeted us very enthusiastically. He would chat and soon he was asking, "How are you feeling? How are you doing with your work?," and other, more personable questions. It was his way. He was very friendly. That's how we started to identify most with Father Stanley, because we could see the work he was doing in the church.

Father Stanley saw our needs. He dedicated himself to helping the people of surrounding communities build houses for widows. He supported students so they could pursue specific careers in other parts of the country. If a young man came to him and said, "Look, Father, I have nothing to study with, I have no way to go, nothing to pay," he would answer, "Come on, I will help you." The only requirement was that he promise to return to town in order to collaborate in some project with the poor. That is how he identified with the people. And he did not think of helping only Catholics. No. He helped whoever was in need.

What he was most enthusiastic about was helping the very poorest people. If someone was quite ill with a disease and looked to him for help, he would say, "Take him to the hospital right away. Take him and then I'll pay for it." And he would pay. Or he himself would go to pay the bills at the Hospitalito. He didn't give the money to the patient, because, frankly, sometimes people, if you give them money, start spending it—or, rather, misspending it. Father Stanley wanted the person to actually get better.

What I saw many times was his desire to talk to people. He had a way of communicating with young people. He clearly enjoyed himself! If he was meeting with a group of people, he started talking to them right away. He was enthusiastic about the culture of Santiago and wanted to keep exploring it further, going deeper into the life of the people. Other missionaries did this too, but not as much as he did. Later, Father Thomas McSherry also entered into the lives of (*convivió con*) many families, but not nearly as much. Father Stanley talked more with the young people. He conversed with everyone. Children would follow him around and hold his hand, both when he entered and when he left mass. He was so eager to try to talk to the children or their parents: "How are you?" and "How are you feeling?" You could sense his kindness. That is why he got invited to have lunch or dinner with the people and their families. He totally identified.

He became so enthusiastic about life in the community that he began to learn Tz'utujil. He wanted to speak Tz'utujil so he could talk to the people in a more intimate way. It was in this way, he thought, that he could communicate the Gospel and the love of God from within our culture. That way he could reach a deeper conversation. That's why I always say, "Padre Apla's really identified with the community!" He became our friend. He conversed with the people. He entered deeply into the culture of the people. He began to feel their problems, feelings, and love so deeply, and all the more because he identified with the people from inside the culture.

Father Stanley was also very practical. I remember a moment a few years later, when the repression of the 1980s was surging. The army imposed a curfew, and it was dangerous to walk about late. But sometimes people didn't know the time, so who knows when they would come home? Being very practical, Father Stanley started to sell cheap watches so that people could come home from work earlier, before the curfew.

He was a hard worker, too. He even liked to work after mass. If he had not had breakfast, he would go to breakfast, but then we would find him working at carpentry in one of the workshops, or he would go to see the construction sites.

In view of his identification with the people, it was not surprising that Father Stanley stayed in Santiago Atitlán when the other priests had already returned to the United States. He stayed and never left. Well, they did convince him to leave Guatemala for a while during the repression, because he had received so many threats. But he could not stand to stay abroad, and he returned. In other words, he never really left us. He could not.

Concerned for the welfare of the people, at one point the Micatokla team raised funds to buy a farm in Panabaj called Cobadonga, which later became an agricultural cooperative. Those in the cooperative worked chicken farms. They sold eggs and vegetables from the farm. Father Stanley grew up in a farming family in Oklahoma, so he loved helping people in the cooperative. Everything he planted there went for distribution among the poor. He also tried out new crops that were not grown here before. Being so practical, when he went to work with the agronomists, he brought down a tractor and was able to improve the harvest. It was another way that he identified with the people.

I remember well Father Stanley's work to replace the church roof a few years after he arrived. The project resulted from his consultations with the elders of both the Atiteco people and of the Catholic community. The mission agreed: "We are going to take out a loan at the bank, and the parish and the community have to raise that money so that you yourselves can build your own church and feel that it is yours." And that's how it worked. A Pro-Reconstruction Committee for the church was formed, of which I was the secretary. Father Stanley coordinated the work, with the help of other priests, and the team of builders. They even helped with the labor—showing how to do it—but we, as a committee, worked with them. Father Stanley, along with Father Robert Westerman, went to great efforts working to help the people. The way they insisted on community participation was excellent.

Most of all, Father Stanley emphasized participation in the catechesis of the mass, with the participation of young people and the participation of women. He held weekly meetings with the catechists, one day a week. He invited people to attend classes on Thursdays, after daily mass. They spent one or two hours commenting on a Gospel text. Father Stanley had a lot of love for all the catechists in each neighborhood. They helped in the celebrations in the neighborhoods where he presided at the Eucharist, and in turn they took the Gospel message to others. Groups were organized in various villages such as Panabaj, Tzanchaj, Chacayá, and on the plantations. Padre Apla's was very interested in the plantations, and in the health of the elderly and children. He would go, even if the road was bad, traveling in his Bronco pickup truck, sometimes alone. He also went to Cerro de Oro to organize the Catholic community there. In the same participatory way that he worked with young people here, he worked in Cerro de Oro, organizing Catholic Action.

In August of 1970, I was appointed director of the radio station. This is the context in which I had the deepest relationship with Padre Apla's. I got to know him much better as parish priest, because we often met as a parish team. As pastor, he would ask how the activities of each coordinator and each commission were going. As the director of the radio station, I had to report how the work was going. I also got involved in catechetical classes, which I attended as a corepresentative from the radio station. Eventually, I began a catechetical radio program. Instead of going to a neighborhood like the other catechists, I went to speak on the radio, doing a religious program. That's the way I worked. I always took what we learned in the classes and broadcast it on the radio.

## APPROACH TO THE *COFRADÍAS*

As time went by, and the Micatokla team shrunk with the departure of other missionaries, Father Stanley was left alone. He had always demonstrated an open attitude towards the *cofradías*. Now that he was left as the only priest, that attitude became more and more important.

In Santiago Atitlán, as in many parts of Guatemala, the *cofradías* maintain certain Maya religious practices in combination with Catholic rites. But the relationship between the *cofradías* and the parish in Santiago is very complex. They were founded by the Spaniards in the old days, to maintain Catholicism through the centuries, because the Church could not keep priests in residence. This was still the situation until the 1940s. They had been organized into twelve individual *cofradías* throughout the community, and each one was well organized. The *cofradías* had always maintained communication with the parish. But they maintained their Maya worldview as well. This could be a source of certain tensions. They always identified themselves as *cofradías* in the first place, even though some *cofradades* held positions in the parish as well. In the decades before Micatokla arrived, tensions had grown.

Previously, during the time when Spanish priests came only once a week to administer the sacraments, my dad was one of the members of Catholic Action. To increase the active presence of the Church in Guatemala, Catholic Action was organized as a lay movement in the 1940s. But it caused a clash, because before that, the *cofradías* had been the ones that supported the church. Historically, they were the ones who maintained the church, so that the Catholic Church would not die.

During that same time period, the Evangelicals started coming in to start their own churches. They wanted to attract more people, saying, "We are better churches—we are not the same as those drunks," and things like that. The Evangelicals objected strongly to the way that the *cofrades* were identified with the Catholic Church. It was a key point of criticism, as they clashed with both the parish and Catholic Action members and their catechists. The Catholics felt somewhat threatened by the arrival of the Evangelical missionaries.

The tension between the parish and the *cofradías* arose around the 1940s, as I understand it. On the one hand, the Catholic Church began to promote Catholic Action to encourage a purer and more orthodox Catholic faith. On the other hand, Evangelicals had shown up with their criticisms of our processions, images of saints, and the importance of Mary. At the same time, Catholic clergy were falling very short in their pastoral practice. That was the time of Spanish priests. As I said, the Spaniards came only to celebrate mass, with no ability to help in social action projects. When there was a celebration of mass, they would finish, and then, "*Adios, ay nos vemos*" [Good-bye, we'll see you], because of the limited time they had to attend to each village.

For both Catholic Action and the Evangelicals, the sin that the *confrades* committed was that they went in processions with a saint while they were *chupando*, as we say, that is, drinking alcohol. They would get drunk while they were with a saint. They had their own rites. So, when Catholic Action got organized with their own catechists, their message was, "You aren't saying the right prayers, so we are going to organize more meetings to pray like good Catholics in church." In fact, the *cofrades* made their prayers through a team of singers under the leadership of an *ajkuun* (Maya priest). The *ajkuun* would say their prayers, and the *cofrades* would follow behind the *ajkuun* in each *cofradía*. The *ajkuun* carries some Maya traditions but has no training in the Gospel.

One also has to recognize that we Maya had our own religions before. It is not that the *cofradías* practiced exactly the same as the ancient Maya. The ancient practices from long ago have been lost, little by little. I have only been talking about what has happened since the 1930s. Much earlier, of course, people had their own celebrations of what is Maya. They identified themselves more with the Maya cosmovision or worldview, but then it got lost. With the formation of the catechists by the Church, and the coming of the Evangelicals, religious leaders in the community clashed among themselves, saying, "You have images, you use your candles, you pray to a saint, not to the true God."

Year after year it became more difficult for the people who wanted to worship God, even if they had different practices and rites, to communicate among themselves. But with the coming of the North Americans, there was a new effort to unite all the leaders of the community to work together for the welfare of the people. The missionaries approached the *cofrades* with love. Sometimes others reacted, asking, "What is this all about?" because they were suspicious. After so many years of division, the invitation, "Let them all come," was a shock to some people. But in this way, the missionaries were successful at entering into the culture with a new kind of evangelization, which included social action projects.

Father Stanley did not bring baggage from all our history of clashes. He found ways to identify himself with others more easily, saying to the cofrades, "You have gotten alienated, so come." He invited them to work together. Even more than other priests in Micatokla, he wanted to enter into their cultural context from the beginning. And once he became our parish priest, he reached out even more. Whether communicating at a distance or relating directly as pastor, he tried to learn their needs. He even provided some financial support for some of their own activities as cofradías.

The main thing that Father Stanley always insisted on from the cofrades—I remember this very clearly—was that they should attend mass on Sundays. They would gather in front of the church and wait for Father Stanley. He would show up in his vestments for mass. Then they would start walking in the procession. They went first; then, with the children of the parish accompanying him, they processed together until they reached the altar, every Sunday. This increased trust and made everyone more enthusiastic about helping each other in little ways. Sometimes he would sit down at the end of the mass to talk, to hear them talk, to hear what they had to say. As he was gradually learning Tz'utujil, he began to speak to them in their first language. In this way he identified himself more than other priests had. He identified directly with the cofradías, and all the cofradías felt more enthusiasm for him—more affection, more friendship.

Once he had entered into the culture, Padre Apla's was able to ask the cofrades to practice the catechism and to participate in the sacraments of the church. Some did and some did not. As a result, some of the same cabeceras and companions began to accept positions in the church, as communion ministers, serving the Catholic people, while still in the cofradías. And to give communion, they first had to be married. "I will get married in the church," one decided, and then, two or three more. They married and received their positions in the parish.

Thanks to the activities that Father Stanley promoted in the town, the cofradías felt a deep friendship with him, and wanted to give him a sign of gratitude. So they themselves placed upon him the sign of a xq'ajkoj, which is a wide cloth woven by hand by the women, containing Maya figures, functioning more or less like a stole placed around the neck. If you look, all the cofrades always have theirs and carry them. It is a sign that identifies them as belonging to their cofradía. They said to Father Stanley, "You are the priest and you identify with us. Thank you for supporting us. We are going to leave you this sign of confraternity." Father Stanley thanked them and from that time on he always carried it to meetings, to mass, everywhere, until his death. He always took his xq'ajk'oj along, because they were the ones who had conferred it upon him. Thus we saw a greater improvement in the relationship between the parish and the *cofradías*.

I myself am not a member of a *cofradía*. They do have some weaknesses, I would say, but they were willing to cooperate. Unfortunately, now they even have conflicts and competition among themselves. They have changed the way they appoint their leaders, so they can keep their positions longer, along with their perks.

The organization of the *cofradías* is not as unified or cohesive as it once was. They maintain their practices, but the organization of community festivities is not like before. Nowadays sometimes they show up, and sometimes they don't. Before, a *cofradía* was responsible for a saint in each neighborhood, and they always made sure they got to church, and they went to mass weekly. Now they hardly do it anymore.

Whatever the weaknesses of the *cofradías* today, I regret that the friendly relationship that Father Stanley maintained with them is no longer in evidence.

## "SMELL LIKE THE SHEEP"

Pope Francis often told priests, bishops, and even cardinals that as shepherds they should "smell like the sheep," that is, get close to and identify with their flock, so much so that they share the same "odors," the same sentiments. That seems to me to be a good way to name the practice of the Micatokla missionary team—most of all, the practice of Father Stanley. For us he remains Padre Apla's, the affectionate name we gave him in Tz'utujil, because he did achieve such identification.

When I heard Pope Francis say that the missionary must enter deeply into the culture of the people, I was elated. Why? Because it reflects the great work that Padre Apla's did in those years of the 1960s and 1970s. I believe that he had the same idea in his mind and in practice as Pope Francis. In those times, as a missionary, he began to enter into the culture of the people. He learned to speak Tz'utujil. He learned to know the elders of the church, insisting that we had to respect each other in the way we worked—not through fights, not through divisions.

This can teach us today, if young people will listen. How to make change? A young person has to do more than follow the changing fads that attract them. They need to learn how true Christians have worked before, and little by little to find a better way. How can we have good communication with others, practicing the Gospel that God wants for us? Not through divisions, but by understanding the life of the people within the culture that already exists. First, understand the culture of each community, because no community is exactly what we think at first. Those who live in Cerro de Oro or those who live in Chacayá or those who are on the plantations—they all have their different needs and perceptions. They don't necessarily think like we do here in Santiago Atitlán. They have other needs, but that shouldn't stop us from working together.

On the plantations, to this day, they have very serious problems—lack of economic resources, lack of health care, lack of many resources. Every people, every community, has its own characteristics. Whether you are a missionary or a social promoter, you have to understand the local dynamics in order to be able to preach and live the Gospel, and not go and divide them. Sometimes the plantation owners don't want you to talk about the people's living conditions. The landowners only want the priest to celebrate mass, baptize, and do a blessing with their holy oil, without other activities that show solidarity with the people. We know that in Guatemala you can't talk openly about a lot of things. They let Father Stanley on to their plantations. But touch their nerves? Preach about sensitive matters? That was another matter.

Father Stanley did not have any direct clashes with the plantation owners because he had a very big heart. His priority was to help the suffering people. I remember once when he found some very sick people on one of the plantations—a woman and a man with their child. He brought them from the plantation and gave them lodging in the parish. Then he sent them to a health center. He found the father a little job he could do at the nutrition center. He had this passion to serve, not only in this case, but in many others.

That is why Father Stanley wanted to continue entering the plantations. Matters were delicate at that time and continue to be so in Guatemala. He was careful not to confront the plantation owners directly about their treatment of their workers, but he did address these things through his biblical reflections at mass. In that way, he was very clear to all the Christians who heard him. He did everything possible for the welfare of others, searching for ways to help. But what could he do alone? What could he do? He asked the catechists to accompany him. Broad support from the whole Church was needed. He alone could not solve all the injustices. But he did what he could with the church's resources. He pastored and did all he could. There was never any doubt that he felt the pain and the burden of our people.

The lesson for us today is that we have to understand each other. If we really want God to enter into us and move our hearts to feel like Christians, we have to make every effort to understand each other. I am talking about the way we should feel when we understand the way of Jesus. If I do not understand my baptism, it is difficult to understand my neighbor. And if I do not reach out to my neighbor, I do not understand my baptism. To follow in the footsteps of Jesus is to fulfill his commandments as Christians, as peoples, until we are even reaching out to the international community, rejecting wars, and showing solidarity in order to build peace.

Blessed Father Stanley "Apla's" Rother accompanies the people in a Good Friday procession. (Courtesy of the Archives of the Archdiocese of Oklahoma City.)

# CHAPTER 4

# For the common good of the people

EVER SINCE I WAS young I felt a drive to get involved in crafts and coopera-tive groups. I enjoyed the work, and it gave me more ideas as to how to work with people. I went to the municipality of San Pedro to learn to weave on large looms. I was involved when the Asociación Voz de Atitlán formed, a professional association for the radio station. While I was learning to weave, I went to the radio station in the afternoons.

In that organization we were thinking about how to help the young and the elderly. We were very concerned, because we saw that people did not know how to read and write, which increased their poverty. We wanted to collaborate somehow—to at least do *something*, even if it would not be a total solution. In 1965 we started teaching. I was 16 or 17 years old. Being very young, I needed to start by working with others. We played sports with other young people, but we got to know each other even better in the jobs we did. We had experienced hard work on the coast, so we looked for alternatives. We started thinking and guiding people to learn new trades and improve our own crops here in Atitlán.

In this way I got more involved, and in 1966–67 we began to organize ourselves for literacy work. The hope was that the people themselves would help us and that they would help their own people. The parish facilitated this work, helping us organize and supporting the program. They also helped with the expenses we needed to project ourselves through radio.

## MY FORMATION

Of course, I was already involved in the parish. When I was 11 years old, I had been an altar boy for priests at mass. I liked it and my dad encouraged me. He took us to mass because my dad was Catholic. Besides being an altar boy, I was a security guard at church. Then, since I already knew how to read and write, I also started helping people to say prayers—reading out loud from the catechism books and translating the homilies of the priests at mass from Spanish into Tz'utujil. Those were the jobs I had been able to do since I was young.

In the beginning, the youth groups were not formal organizations. There was nothing like that in Santiago Atitlán, either in the community or the parish. Before 1966 the only formal organizations were the Catholic church and one Evangelical church, the Iglesia Centroaméricana. But a few years after the arrival of Micatokla, the Oklahoma mission began to help and support young people. They formed a soccer team. Still, these were just small groups, with no formal organization. The first organization to be formalized was the radio station, because of the need for authorization under the Ministry of Communications and the Ministry of Education. It was a requirement that we be well organized, with legal status, bylaws, and a board of directors. When agricultural and handicraft cooperatives were formed, it was also more formal. Youth groups simply functioned under the umbrella of the church.

The Micatokla mission was quite important for the personal formation of many young people, including myself. No other organization in Santiago helped the youth, either in recreation, education, jobs, family matters, or any other activity. There was simply nothing else. Micatokla was the first organization to arrive in those years to support the general population in every way. When the North Americans arrived, they brought many programs. They brought crafts, painting, guitar and other music lessons, sculpture, carpentry. They looked for opportunities so that children and young people could do some form of recreation.

As I have already said, in Santiago before the arrival of the North Americans, there was a population full of children, but many of them died. Why did they die? Because of malnutrition and disease. The main diseases were tuberculosis, measles, and pulmonary diseases. Malnutrition robs children of their strength. And as children, we mostly played in the dirt, unsupervised, making crude toys out of sticks, in a not-so-healthy way—if we had time to have fun at all. Frequently, children accompanied their fathers to work, as I explained in a previous chapter. Children were vulnerable in many ways. So there was a lot of sickness – so very much sickness.

That is why the first major investment the mission made was in health centers with nurses. They hired a team of Guatemalan and North American doctors. They brought in vaccines. Vaccines are what helped many, many children. We started to feel like salvation was coming! For many people, the chance to recover life had arrived! As people began to accept the vaccines, they saw that fewer children died. Of course, at the beginning, some people did not accept them. Many feared that they brought evil, because they thought, "I don't know who sent me this help, and I don't know where it came from! Who is it? Who are they? I am surprised to see new, tall people with white faces." People were surprised and wary at the beginning, but when they saw the improvement in the health of those who were vaccinated, confidence grew.

The goal of Micatokla was that the people themselves organize and support each other. With the initiative of the missionaries, the parish and the community were organized in commissions—for education, health, recreation, scholarships, support to the children, support to the youth, visits to the elderly. We saw all this as a great salvation. The very way that they had arrived and proceeded to work was communicating the very human dignity by which God created us and continues seeking to restore every human being.

The arrival of the Micatokla team encouraged me personally more and more in my own growing social commitment. After all that I had already seen in the hard work on the coast and in my life, the fact that they had arrived was a call and opportunity to collaborate. I had seen the problems of my people on the coast and in the suffering people in neighborhoods, villages, and municipalities of our Atiteca region. It was a frustration not to be able to come to people's aid. But then I saw that the missionaries were organizing commissions to address these needs.

My growing concern was how I could join these social programs. One cannot do much acting alone. So I got involved. I liked the atmosphere on the projects. I learned a little bit about each project and each job, and I was constantly encouraging other people too, saying, "Come, come! Don't be afraid!" and "You should find out. Do what the doctors recommend." To the sick I'd say, "Go to the hospital. There is a health center, there is medicine, there are doctors. I'll go with you if you want!" And if some were still afraid, "Come on, young people! To recreation! To play! Come on, guys!" The projects were fun, and I wanted to participate in health programs, though without discouraging the use of the herbal medicines that our elders had passed down.

Sometimes I came home very late. Why? From going around and talking to people. It was necessary to tell them in their own language. Because when other people arrived speaking Spanish, many didn't understand. Social promoters have to speak the language of the people. Imagine the arrival of mission workers, if they want to do evangelization and only speak Spanish! The people did not understand them. If they spoke Spanish and the people spoke Tz'utujil, they wouldn't understand. Today, it is still like that. I remind foreigners to learn to understand our language. If there are 100 older people, 20 or 30 are not going to understand Spanish. Only the young people who have been to school will understand.

So you see the need to enter directly into the culture of the people. As much as the people need work, livelihood, vaccinations, health care, and recreation for the youth and children, nothing can be done without entering into the culture. Especially in the first years of Micatokla, the mission needed promoters who could understand them and at the same time explain how our culture worked. The missionaries did not speak any Tz'utujil at first, because they had just come. And you can't learn the language very fast. But in a few years, yes, they started. In the meantime, the priests were putting together their team in the parish.

In short, because of my experiences as a child and young man, I had a yearning to help people, and suddenly the opportunity appeared. I rushed to get involved in social projects, because there was a need that I had already seen in the community.


## ROOTS OF MY SOCIAL COMMITMENT

As for the roots of my social commitment, I feel that it came from my parents' values. Life was hard for my parents. They were both orphans who lost their parents when they were three or four years old. My dad hung in there and did everything he could to support the family and improve their conditions. My mom was also lucky to find ways to survive in life. She didn't give up; she fought to do something. I have three brothers and sisters who unfortunately still can't read and write, and they are already quite old. Thus I know a lot about people going through these struggles—the feelings of each one and the relationships among them. I felt this same feeling of struggle and desire to do something with my life. I am grateful that I learned how to use various means of communication as a tool to promote good conduct in our community. On the one hand, that is how to learn what people need. And on the other, that is how one learns to grow in life.

The grit that I had needed on the coast and in other work settings, along with my friends, joined together with the spirit of my childhood, and gave me a heart for other people. Since I was a child, I had been encouraged to listen to the preaching of many people about the word of God. What stood out to me were the words about how it is so good to help and work with each other, cooperating with each other. Then in my youth I thought, "What can I do in life when I am older? How can I contribute through my work, my life, and in my family?"

One should not think only of oneself. Many people—let's admit it, sometimes we ourselves—once we have a house, we want five more houses. And from that comes the temptation to exploit others. I somehow found the courage to tell myself, "I have an adequate house. So how can I help other people, children, and young people? I can accompany others in development projects. I can contribute with my work, with my testimony, with my personal activities in life. I am going to analyze how I have solved my own problems and conflicts in order to encourage others. That's how I found myself saying to the people, "Look, here's what I've found to work. Let's help each other. Let's join together." That's the way to work enthusiastically in groups and organizations. As we worked that way and felt the support of the mission, we found greater strength to mutually help one another.

Of course, there are many people who hear the word of God and continue to think only of themselves. I don't have it in my head to know why. What I have sensed is what God has given me, the character I was born with. I think a lot of our people—including myself, sometimes—hear good examples, good readings, good preaching, but we just listen. We get the words in our heads, but the words don't penetrate into our hearts. There is a mismatch. Because a lot of people—even ourselves sometimes, most of us in the world—study, but it just warms our heads. A lot of things fill our heads. But when it comes to putting things into practice with our neighbor, our hearts stay empty.

Working for others can certainly be a bit costly: working, helping, walking together, accompaniment, finding time, kindness—a lot of things are necessary. And sometimes you have to leave your home and your family to attend meetings. We may not want to, but it is necessary to carry out what we have heard from the word of God. Listening to doctrine is nice, but if it stays in the head, and does not fall into our hearts, it is not enough. Love for other persons involves the heart, right? I can't say, "I am only going to think. Yes, what Jesus said was good! Great, in fact." Or we say, "I'll contribute. I'll listen to a lecture. I'll do something good. At the university they told me such-and-such." Yes, they told you. But are you ready to roll up your sleeves and go to work? It's often difficult for us because of demands on our time. We say, "I have other obligations and commitments. I have a very big job. I can't do what God wants me to do."

Every time we were at mass, especially after these missionaries arrived, the priests tried to get this message across. Sometimes they preached one way, sometimes another—softer, slower, or bit by bit, but always well. When we were children, they told us not to fight, not to hit others. If you have a little bit of food, give a little bit to the other person. And my dad taught me that too, from childhood on. I remember well.

## THE WISDOM OF THE ELDERS

My maternal grandfather had a lot of influence on me too. There were three of us grandsons who lived near him. He took us to the fields to work. My grandfather had no religion. He didn't go to the *cofradía* or to the Catholic church or to an Evangelical church. He did go to church to kneel and pray at times, but more often he prayed when he took us to the fields.

When we arrived, he would tell us, "Please don't cut down any trees just for fun. Don't cut the trees. They are our companions, because God has given us life. Please!" Upon our arrival, we placed our little bags on a bush or tree; then he would make us kneel down and ask God's permission first: "You are our true owner, the owner of the world, the owner of our body, who has given us life." There was no preaching, no noise, but we felt the presence of God. He was an old man, already 70 years old when I was maybe seven or eight. He would tell us, "Look, you are going to do what I say. Listen to the birds. They're singing. They're singing to God. What about you? Do you just come in here and cut whatever you want? No. That tiny bird eats grass, fruits, and that's why it sings. So, we are going to kneel down and ask permission to the Supreme Being, the owner of the world."

And so he continued, praying, "Lord, we ask permission because we are going to start using the hoe. We are going to kill the weeds, pulling them up, with your permission. We are going to weed, and we are going to sow our corn, our beans. And Lord, please give us a little bit of water, to water our crop a little bit. My grandchildren are here with me. May they learn everything you want them to learn. Always give us good knowledge, not to fight and not to accept harmful words. So often we hurt each other. Forgive us. Excuse us, yes, please excuse us. Just as we are going to start working now, so we want to return to our home. May nothing bad happen to us on the way." And if he had some incense, my grandfather would start to light some candles. In those days he did not know Spanish, much less how to read and write, but he was very kind and sincere in his prayers, asking for the common good of his children and the community.

When I got home, it was the same thing. At dawn, the same thing. Whenever we started eating, we all got together, and my grandfather would say, "Let's give thanks for our food." Before we started, he would say, "Let's give thanks. Who gave us this food? The Supreme Being, because he gave us life through nature. We have corn. We have everything. Our Mother Earth prepares all her work. We are collaborators with the Supreme Being. Collaborators! We are not owners. He has lent us everything. So we must collaborate and be grateful."

That's what he used to say. How beautiful were my grandfather's prayers! I knew him very well. He always wore typical Maya garb and a palm leaf hat, all neat and proper. He lived in a little straw house. With the advice he gave us, I believe that he sowed in his grandchildren the values of my parents and elders. Unfortunately, he was the only grandparent I knew. If I had known my other grandparents, they too would have been my best teachers, as he was.

I said that my grandfather had no religion, but that's not exactly correct. Maybe my grandfather went to mass only a few times, because there were not many masses in our town in the old days. There was no Catholic organization in that time, because there was no opportunity. It is not that he was anti-Catholic. But he definitely had a very deep Maya spirituality. It makes sense, because where else could all those things come from that he said in his prayers? His values and sentiments went very deep. He had heard them much earlier from his own parents. He had learned them in that same way. That really is the Maya religion that has come from long, long before.

My grandfather had another lesson for us too: "If you see a person who is kneeling in front of a stone, or if he is kneeling in front of a tree, or if he is kneeling on a hill, leave him alone, because he is talking to his God. Leave him. Don't interfere. Every person knows why and when to give their own thanks to the world and their Creator for the gifts they have received. Look around. Observe. Just don't judge. Who knows who is doing wrong or doing right? I cannot see. I cannot judge." That's what he was saying. A lot of people these days go around yelling up and down the street—and I don't try to stop them. Because I can't judge. I can't say who that is or what is the true religion.

Still, I am convinced of this: The true Christian for me is the one who fulfills the word of God with his neighbor. That's what I can say. Because God wants us to hear it, then put it to work through our life. That's what I can say.

## ESCAPE FROM THE MILITARY RESERVE

Since he was an orphan, my father got taken to the military barracks here in the Department of Sololá and was a soldier during the time of Jorge Ubico, the Guatemalan president from 1931 to 1944. My father was in the barracks for eight years. He became a second lieutenant. When he came back, he married my mom, had a family, and loved us very much. He worked for our good, to give us food. However, wages were very low. He didn't like working here in town, because the pay was so bad. So he started doing small jobs, carrying loads to sell in other municipalities. It was grueling work. But he accompanied people to church and became a Catholic. He was a member of Catholic Action and collaborated with the Pro-Reconstruction Committee of the church in the 1940s. When we were born, he was already a Catholic, and he took us to church. That's how we got started. He was very responsible among the people in the church.

I remember that when I was young, they began to press young men to serve in the military reserves here. They were taking young people to start doing exercises and enter the military, led by a colonel and a lieutenant. I didn't really understand what was going on. I was just hanging around with the young men. I said, "It's cool that they are doing these exercises. I like it! Let's go see, let's go!" We went to see, and they grabbed me to join the group. I attended the training that first Sunday and then a second Sunday.

My dad realized that I had gotten involved in this. He scolded me at home: "You were supposed to ask permission before you got involved in things like this. I've spent most of my life in those jobs. I don't want you to be a soldier. I have seen and known what that life is all about. Besides, you are only 17 years old. You're not going to leave, I'm not going to let you leave." After he scolded me, he left at once to talk to the colonel.

He told the colonel, "Let my son stay out of the reserves." The colonel asked him, "Why?" And he replied, "I know why. I know the soldier's life. I know military life. I don't want him to have any part of it." They started arguing, until finally the colonel said to my dad, "Well, your son gets out. But you remain on call, because there is no one to play the snare drum. You know how. You learned that in the barracks. You are going to teach the young people." My father said: "Okay, I'll do what you want, but not my son. He is a minor." So he stayed in and took me out, while he taught the young people how to drum, how to march—all the exercises that young men do. He stayed on himself but took me out.

## LEARNING TO COLLABORATE WITH THE PEOPLE

Our first social promotion project in the communities began in 1965 and continued while we built a building for the radio station. We worked with young people in all the municipalities. I also organized cooperatives in other municipalities of San Antonio Palopó and Santa Catarina Palopó. We constructed a building for the radio station, always collaborating with the Catholic Church. Father Stanley was pastor during that time, and we got to know each other very well in the midst of his work.

After his death in 1981, it was a hard time for us. I stayed shut up in my house because they were looking for us. Then, in 1983 and 1984, I had the opportunity to study and earn a teaching degree. In 1983 I was given an opportunity to work with children in Cerro de Oro. When I started working there, I began to see the needs that existed in the community.

The elementary school went only to the third grade. For fourth, fifth, and sixth, the children had to travel to San Lucas Tolimán. The children had to walk three kilometers or more in the rain to get there. I decided to ask the parish priest of San Lucas, Monsignor Gregory Schaffer, for help. I asked him to please help us finance teachers so that the children from Cerro de Oro could complete sixth grade right there in the school. I explained that we had a school, but no teachers. Father Gregory responded favorably. He helped fund a number of projects there that benefited children, including a preprimary program. He authorized two or three more teachers and, after a couple of years, a request was made to the Ministry of Education to continue financing up to sixth grade.

Another need in the community was for clean drinking water. The people of Cerro de Oro went to the lake for water, and it was quite a distance. I asked a local man named Juan Cotzal if he could help us determine what we needed and whom to ask for help. I would need the collaboration of people who would donate pumps, pipes, accessories, and everything necessary to bring water to the community of Cerro de Oro. As a teacher, I had already asked one of the plantations to collaborate with us, and they gave us a pump, pipes, and two tanks that are still there next to the Catholic church.

Through efforts like these, I learned how to collaborate with the people. They were totally amazed when the water was inaugurated. The municipal authorities had not been able to get any support. The initiative had come entirely from the community. We worked on it ourselves. The community threw a party to celebrate. They roasted chickens and prepared a lot of food because the water had arrived. It was a very nice event!

In that same year, 1985, I was president of Catholic Action in the parish, and I had to think about how to proceed and organize group activities. Those were the years when the soldiers were frequently in the fields looking for guerrillas, but many *campesinos* did not speak Spanish and had trouble communicating with the authorities. Because of misunderstandings, both sides—the guerrillas and the army—could threaten the *campesinos* and even kill them. For that reason, there was even more need for education. But there was only one school in town. I wondered what was going to happen to the children in the future, the children who needed education. I had been in school since I was very young and had only a few grades to show for it. The same thing was going to happen to the children of this new generation. There was only one school with about 10 to 12 teachers in this whole population.

Since I was already a teacher, I began to think about founding a school in each neighborhood of Santiago Atitlán to see what would happen. But what should I do? How to move forward? Whom do I talk to? Well, I decided to begin by going to talk to the people themselves—the people of each community. There are five communities here, five "cantons" or neighborhoods in Santiago. I started thinking and talking to the president of Catholic Action in each one. They came up with ideas for how to get schools in each community.

Ha! It was sweet bread for them. "Yes, we have kids, we have kids, we want schools ourselves!" Everyone offered opinions and ideas. Some were fighting for my allegiance, asking why I wasn't going to do school in their neighborhood, and so on. I had to tell them, "Yes, of course. Just let me think about what we need to do, who to talk to, how to organize ourselves, what house we are going to use."

"Ah, no problem," they would answer, "we can get a house from the brothers or the friends of so and so." I remember it all quite clearly. Here in Pachicháj we went to visit with an old man, a *cofrade* with the last name of Ruíz. That year it was not his turn to host the *cofradía* meetings, so I asked if we might use his house for the school. I told him, "Look, it is going to be a service for the children and the teachers." He responded enthusiastically, "Thank you, don Juan. Thank you because you want to open this little house for the children, and so do I. Use the house!" He didn't charge us anything; it was totally free. Afterwards, the girls' organization, the Daughters of Mary, offered to provide snacks for the children. The parents came and helped clean the house. In another neighborhood, Panaj, the elderly lady Dolores Pablo lent us her house as a form of collaboration.

What were the steps to start a school? The first step was the house, that is, where to teach. Second was the supervisor, whether or not he would give his permission to start the five schools. I told him all about the five communities.

He told me, "Let's go see if there is room. We're going to see if there are students." I assured him that there were plenty of students.

"But teachers?" he asked me. "There are no teachers. If we apply today to the Ministry of Education, that will take another year."

"It's okay," I explained. "We're working on that. But first we need you to get on board. Do you authorize, or don't you authorize?"

"Yes, I will authorize it."

Next, I thought, "Now I'll look for funding for one or two teachers in each neighborhood." I went to talk to Father Thomas McSherry in 1985. I said, "Look, Father, let me tell you about my idea. I was in Cerro de Oro working with children, and the thought came to me—I want a school in each neighborhood of Santiago. The people are willing. They are ready to lend out their houses. In Pachicháj we will use the house of a *cofrade*. In Panáj there is a house of a widow who will not charge us. In Tzajuyú they will lend us two rooms in a private house. In Panúl we will use the house of the Micatokla mission, because there is a house that you have bought. And in Xechivoy we are thinking of using the parish house."

Father Thomas said to me, "Of course, use it! I like that you're doing this! I like the community involvement!" he told me. "I like the idea, Juan, I really like it. But what does the supervisor say?" I explained that the supervisor had authorized the project if we could get the funds.

That's how I lobbied Father Thomas with a bit of banter. "No problem," he said, "I can cover salaries for two teachers in each neighborhood for two years, while you apply for permanent funds from the Ministry of Education." I was almost in tears from the joy, from all my emotions.

Once I knew that the priest would authorize the funds, I went back to tell the supervisor that we had the money for the teachers. The supervisor went to each neighborhood to draw up documents for the operation of each school, according to the requirements of the Ministry of Education. Several teachers were hired to work in each one. The supervisor offered to transfer an experienced teacher to the Panúl neighborhood, Professor Héctor Roderico Guzmán. He was the first director there. That young man had a passion and an ability to work with the community, with the children. What a good teacher! With his help the school grew quickly.

So that is how each of the schools in each neighborhood was founded. The departmental director of education at that time was Francisco Puac. He communicated with the teachers and said, "We have to transfer professor Juan Ajtzip from Cerro de Oro to the official school of the Panúl neighborhood in Santiago. He deserves this transfer, because he helped found five schools in Santiago. We want to reward him by having him work in one of them." In truth, the project was the achievement of many people in each community who wanted to collaborate and work to educate the children. Everywhere we had worked, people wanted to collaborate. And collaborate they did.

There was only one problem. The people of Cerro de Oro did not want me to leave their community as a teacher. They were angry because I was being transferred to Santiago. They came to my house with an official from Cerro de Oro and said, "We are going to remove the supervisor, because we did not like that he removed you as teacher." Still, they thanked me for having collaborated with the community in their projects, especially with the community committees.

So I organized and worked, collaborating with the communities. Elders, men, women, youth, boys, girls—together we had all elaborated the objectives of the project. And I had learned from them how to work together.

Now in the 2020s there are from 10 to 15 teachers in each neighborhood. There has been a lot of growth. When I see the many children here in town or in the countryside, or when we have a festival with parades, it makes me reflect on all these experiences. As long as I am alive, seeing children will give me joy, as I remember what Jesus helped me to do through my life.

Bishop Eusebio Beltrán of Tulsa (and later Oklahoma City) with Juan Ajtzip and his son Luis, and Father Thomas McSherry, in the late 1990s. (Courtesy of Juan Ajtzip.)

# CHAPTER 5

# Integral evangelization

WHAT SHOULD BE CLEAR by now is that the conception of evangelization that motivated Father Stanley—Padre Apla's—and the other missionaries of Micatokla was something that they had to manifest in their practical lives, as well as in their preaching. Spirituality was visible in their willingness to serve the community. Padre Apla's showed his kindness by sharing his life (*convivencia*) with the youth groups, the children, the elderly, and the families. He tried to meet the needs of each family. He encountered the sick and their illnesses; he met the blind and those who could not walk. Upon his arrival, he saw that there was no hospital and that there was no way to help people get better. Without some improvement in their lives, it would be difficult to preach the word of God. Sick people were not going to listen very well! "I want your body to be well," he told them, "so you can really hear me."

## THE PRACTICE OF LOVE

When Father Stanley sent people to be cured and paid for their medicines, he didn't leave people in the middle of their problems. He followed their cases until they got better. And he never asked about the person's religion; he helped whoever was in need.

That is the love that Padre Apla's lived out among the people, show-ing the charity of the Gospel by his use of the alms that the church had collected and the resources of Micatokla. From the very beginning, he was friendly to anyone who visited the church. If any group invited him over to chat in the evening, he would go. And if they gave him dinner, he would eat whatever they offered. He liked *patín*, the traditional dish of our town.[1] He liked the *tamalitos*, but only if they were very clean, because sometimes it made him sick! At times he did get sick eating the local food, but he always accepted our hospitality.

Father Stanley's conception of evangelization was evident in his commitment to working totally from the words of Jesus. He expressed many aspects of the Gospel, and of the life and words of Jesus, simply by being with the people, with the poor, with the needy. He made sure that the Gospel was integrated both with the body of the human being and with the spirituality that we need. He believed that Jesus had not come just to talk and observe the pains of the people, only to say good-bye. No. Jesus did miracles. Jesus worked with the people. He multiplied the bread. He gave sight to the blind and health to the lame, to everyone.

He was a priest who was always looking for ways to help. He was ready to draw upon medical science if that could cure other people's pain. He encouraged parents to educate their children and young people to understand their parents, both as an act of love. He patiently explained to parents, "To improve your condition in life will show love to your children and bring greater unity to your family."

God's love was always evident in the way that Padre Apla's approached us. Because he lived so closely with us, he also experienced our faults and conflicts directly, when we fought with each other. There are always quarrels, after all. Why do they exist? There are conflicts over land, over wanting more, to the point of stealing from others. Why? Because of the vices of money. We end up going to a judge or a court to see who wins and who loses. That is not the love of God. The way of God's love is to go to your neighbor to say, "Look. What has happened? Maybe we didn't understand each other." And from there, "Yes, we were wrong, but let's reconcile." Father Stanley used that word often: reconcile.

In fact, he went directly to work on behalf of reconciliation; he didn't just talk about it at mass. He talked with families about their conflicts, asking, "What is going on here?" He wasn't like some of the preachers we see shouting in the park. Instead, he went from house to house, visiting—in families, meeting the young people. In every meeting he conducted, in

---

1. *Patín* consists of a mixture of tomato paste and meat or very small fish from Lake Atitlán, which has been salted and dried. All this is wrapped in *maxán* leaf.

every talk he gave, at baptisms, at marriages, with catechists, he used the opportunity to cultivate human relationships.

That's why Father Stanley also liked that we used the radio as a means to evangelize. Through his talks, he had been forming us, so that we too could share the Gospel. We were his students, and still are. Of course, if someone has fifty students, they are not all going to learn the same thing. We are all different. That's why Padre Apla's tried so hard to enter into the hearts of the people. How else were they going to understand? How else could he communicate?

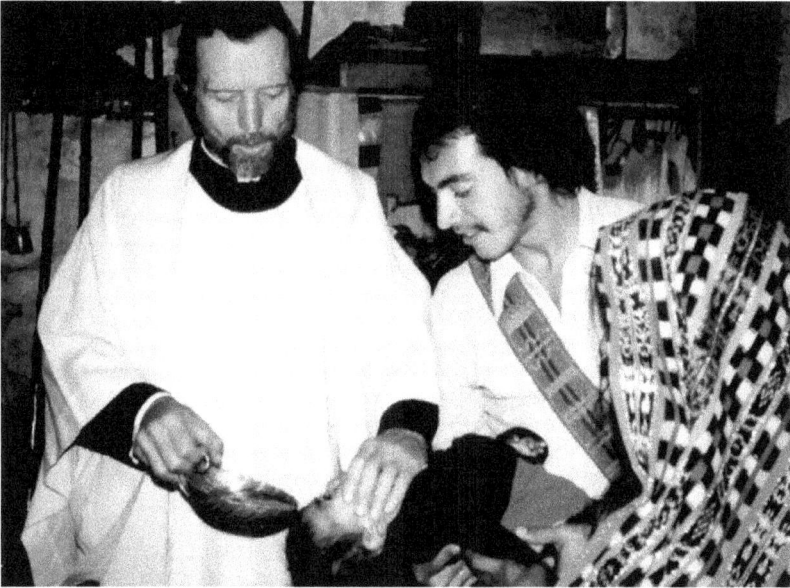

Father Stanley Rother and a deacon baptizing a child.
(Courtesy of the Archives of the Archdiocese of Oklahoma City.)

Here again we see the importance of using the Tz'utujil language. That's why Padre Apla's began to learn. He was already saying, "*Melti'oox!*" (Thank you!) more than the other priests. I did not see them speak in Tz'utujil. They might try a few words. But he went deeper. He followed through that way. By learning and speaking Tz'utujil, he manifested his charity, his love for our people. He said, "I am not leaving here. I am staying here." He said it constantly: "These are my people."

I believe that all those who came here through Micatokla as missionaries were motivated to work well in the service of others. We know that not everyone has the same desire to serve. Often we make excuses. We need to understand what Jesus tells us in his Gospel: what it is to love, what it is to forgive, what it is to express affection for another person. Father Stanley had this sensibility, and he expressed the Spirit of God in his heart by being and living here in Santiago Atitlán, rather than living a much more comfortable life in his own country. He wanted to live among a people where he was needed.

According to the Bible, Jesus did it in this same way. He demonstrated love and affection for others. This is what I believe motivated Padre Apla's. It could be that, if he were still alive, he would tell us why he came here and how he was able to give so much of himself. But short of that, I cannot penetrate his heart. What I could understand, I understood through his life actions. He listened. He paid attention to those who were hungry, to those who were sad, to those who had problems, to those who were homeless, to those left out in the rain. This is what Padre Apla's manifested to us. He helped widows, orphans, and students.

## TEACHINGS OF LOVE

I recall how these themes came up in Father Stanley's teachings and preaching, as I look back after so many years. He preached that we should demonstrate this same love of God with our neighbors, showing mutual love. That is what he always said, not to hate one another. He felt that in the town of Santiago there was no reason for major clashes. What the priests sought to do through their evangelization was to deepen our Christian life together (*convivencia cristiana*). That is what he wanted, that we love each other and understand the word of God. He told us to live more as brothers and sisters, to deepen our friendships, demonstrating these qualities through our deeds. Families should not be divided, should solve their problems together. At work and in the fields, we should behave well. Young men, women, and children must all behave well, because God wants good for us. Each Gospel gives us examples of what God—what Jesus—preached. He repeated the message many times. I know that is what Father Stanley felt in himself, that through the love of God, he must work with others. After all, this is what he preached in his homilies more than anything else.

In his preaching from the Gospels, Father Stanley almost always emphasized the practical examples that touched our own lives and our deeds. Whenever we heard a Gospel reading, he would ask us, "What is it saying about our lives?" He told us, "Understand. Use your heart. Be for others." So as soon as we heard, we were supposed to follow the examples, and do so with our deeds. That's what he was working toward. He didn't want merely to pass on the words of the Gospels, without putting them into practice on behalf of others. He himself worked the fields. He met with small groups of farmers, and out of what they produced, they too ended up giving a portion to the poor.

This is the love that he taught us. I feel it was God's own love, through the Holy Spirit. The commitment to become a Christian is a commitment to fulfill one's baptism—to fulfill all the sacraments of the church. Some people say, "I don't understand what's going on here. I'd better go to another church." But that's because they did not understand what the Gospel is, what God asks of us. It is not a question of religion; it is a question of understanding one's religion. Padre Apla's always emphasized that, because this was the time when divisions were really deepening here in Atitlán. This was when so many divisions began—divisions between churches, the creation of other churches—which we are still living with today.

I do not want to speak of things that I have not lived out within other churches, because I have not been with them. Jesus' attitude, according to the apostles, was evident when the disciples wanted to scold others who preached and did miracles in his name. Jesus told them not to forbid others, because "whoever is not against us is for us" (Mark 9:40, NRSV). We cannot talk about other groups. If they are doing good, I cannot judge them. Other denominations are helping people too. There are others who are giving help, doing good, not taking advantage of the community. Before God, this is good. And I think that was the attitude of Padre Apla's, because I never saw him discriminating between religions or with the alms of the parish.

## THE INTEGRATION POINT

Among all the projects that Micatokla initiated, the radio station was key. The mission team from Oklahoma was made up not only of priests but also of agronomists, educators, and doctors. Looking at the population, what stood out was the need for literacy. A large number could not read or write at all. They did not speak Spanish either, only Tz'utujil. That is where the team saw so much need for education. From among the catechists, a group was designated to form a literacy team. Education was going to be our responsibility, and soon, as things developed, radio programs would be our main strategy.

We were accompanied by a missionary, Elizabeth Nick, a nun on the Micatokla team. She was in charge of bringing us together and orienting us as to how we could work to help illiterate people. Soon a number of us came to help and to learn with her. She said, "I want to learn how to help the people, and I need your participation. I cannot do it alone. With your collaboration we can open a way. For many people, literacy is the path forward." So we got started.

Every Sunday, Sister Elizabeth began to guide us with training sessions in reading and writing. This is when many people in the community started to learn to read and write. But as soon as they learned, she told them, "Now it is your turn. You must go to your neighborhoods and teach other people. From what I teach you here, you can now teach your family, your children, your grandchildren, and your neighbors. On Sunday we meet; on Monday we work with the community." This is where formal work began. Didactic materials were developed for us to share our work.

Sometimes there was nowhere to meet, so we borrowed classrooms from the public school and from the parish. The teachers laughed at us: "Where did you come from, you people who have no ability to teach?" But we had already learned a method for teaching. As soon as someone learned three letters, they had to teach those three letters to their group in their neighborhood. It was the best way. We took one syllable and went from there! And people accepted this idea.

The pastor at that time (this was before Father Stanley became the pastor) came and said, "Let's use a radio transmitter. Let's stop using the loudspeakers." After all, a loudspeaker reaches only one block at most, maybe from the church to the school. We all lived in the different neighborhoods, many blocks away, and the lessons couldn't reach us there. So he said, "We are going to bring a radio station."

We had to get organized, because to start a radio station, you have to have an assigned frequency. An association was formed, with its statutes, with its legal status, constituting a legal organization. To get started, the Micatokla mission paid for the expenses. They gave us lamps. They gave us teaching materials. By the time they actually imported the transmitter, the group was already organized. The authorities saw that the purpose was for literacy and education. They authorized a transmitter for us without presenting any obstacles. It didn't take long.

It was an old transmitter. Father Stanley said it was from World War II. It was a gift to us. It was 300 watts of power, 120 kilocycles. You couldn't hear it on just any receiver. You needed a special pretuned radio receiver. With that, we started working in the neighborhoods. Sister Elizabeth Nick was the first director of the radio, starting in 1966, but several years later she returned to her country. By the time she left us, Father Stanley was the pastor, and he assured us that he wouldn't abandon the project. He continued to support us.

From the very beginning of the radio station, I was involved in everything. The station's assembly sent me to intern for a year in another educational radio station in Nahualá to gain experience. At the end of 1970 the assembly elected me director of the radio station here. Father Stanley approved, called me, and said, "We know each other well. You will be in charge of running the station, but please cooperate closely with the other groups of people that have also gotten organized." So that is how we Atititcos started to manage the radio ourselves, always with the advice and support of Father Stanley. I participated in weekly meetings with the coordinators of the other local and national parish commissions.

We have always had a board of directors for the radio station. It is not just the director who is in charge. There is an assembly, a board of directors, and its director, all working together. Father Stanley told us to work independently from the parish. However, he always helped us with repairing and starting the generator for the transmitter, while the radio technician was Father Thomas Stafford. If we needed any parts, they encouraged us to ask them to bring them from the United States. Father Stanley always stayed on top of the news that I brought him about how the radio was doing, and about the transmission of masses. That was his commitment.

A few years later, Monsignor Victor Reed, the bishop of Oklahoma City, came and said, "I support the radio. We will continue to collaborate. I will continue to send help for the radio, but you should also look for other alternatives to be able to sustain the radio. Now is the time for you to become independent of the church. You already have your association, and the equipment we have given you. I am ready to sign off." Our bishop in Sololá agreed. That was roughly 1972. "Now, then, you are independent from the church," they said, "but we will continue giving our hand with the transmissions of mass and religious programs. We all agree. We have already prepared everything for you. You must find the best way to proceed. After these years of preparation, you know the way forward."

## ORGANIZED TO WALK TOGETHER

When I started working at the radio, it was as if a tool to help the people had finally been put into our own hands. I had learned from my life experiences, from entering into the life of the people, and from the pain that they bore. I had seen that problems were similar in every community, in every village along the lakeshore. And with this tool we were able to begin to walk, organizing people in literacy centers, coordinating with cooperatives, promoting handicrafts, in the whole area of the Tz'utujil and also of the Kakchiquel.

In 1973–1974 we worked with the board of directors to buy a piece of land and build a building. We worked for about two or three years on the project. We constructed the building for the radio station, doing all the things that the community wanted. Later, we also ran a school and built a two-story building with the collaboration of the community. This was called the *Voz de Atitlán* Intercultural High School, where we taught the children in both Spanish and Tz'utujil. That was also how we did our radio programming. The literacy programs were the same, written in Spanish and Tz'utujil. We also offered programs in Kakchiquel and other Mayan languages.

People really liked having a radio. They were enthusiastic, especially when they heard their own native music. Soon we started hearing people singing songs from the radio in the street. People kept asking for more songs in Tz'utujil. We knew then that we had popular support. The radio station was opening more space for our own culture.

At the national level, we have been members of the Guatemalan Federation of Radio Schools, and I was president of the federation for a few years. We have even been members at the Latin American level. This gave us many contacts and helped us keep developing. I was the director for about 24 years. International relations made it possible to get new transmitters and materials for the construction of the building. We kept groups of people in each local municipality, collaborating in their own towns.

It is worth noting that the management of the station followed the same philosophy of development that we had seen with Micatokla, always based on the participation of the people. Micatokla had rejected a paternalistic philosophy in favor of empowering us to own and manage the projects ourselves. Now we no longer had a priest or a nun on the board of directors. We ourselves were trained, and we continue to train other people in the same way.

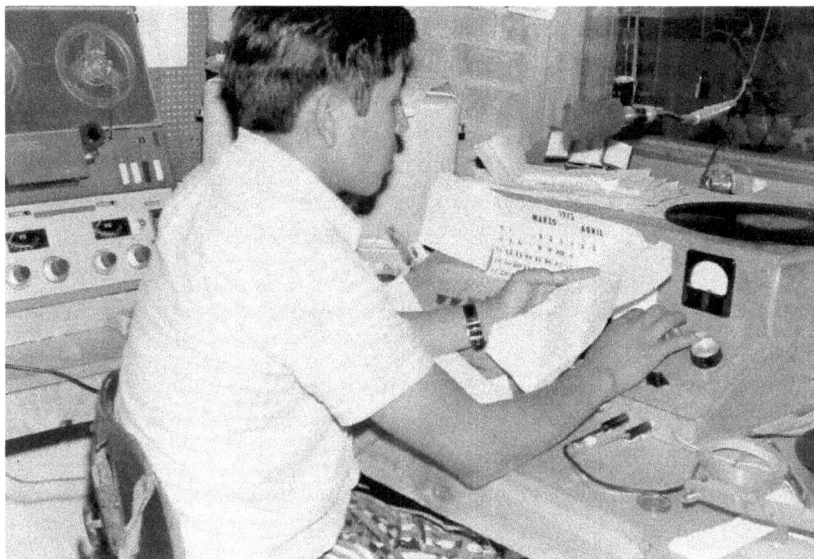

Juan Ajtzip at the Voice of Atitlán radio station, 1970. (Courtesy of Juan Ajtzip.)

The missionaries had had this idea from the beginning. They always told us, "You have a method for how to work, so we want you to manage your own institutions. We support you." We had a lot of people involved, but the elders were the ones who collaborated with us the most. In any project they would say, "Let's do it!"

The radio became a vehicle for other social projects and topics. I remember that, as director, I received support from Caritas Guatemala, through its director in Nahualá. We divided projects up so we could reach people in all the municipalities, both here in Atitlán and in the lakeshore municipalities. We promoted organic fertilizers, taught handicrafts, made loans from Caritas funds, and our colleague Diego Coché managed the project. He was very committed. They even gave him a horse so he could visit the most isolated villages. He did not use a car. He did not use a motorcycle. He just went on horseback, traveling to each village to help. The radio station facilitated all of these projects, announcing meetings and broadcasting our talks. That's why, to this day, the radio and its programs are so integral to community life. The work itself is integral, as it addresses all the spiritual, economic, material, and cultural dimensions of life.

That is the work we have done. Many accepted it, although a few rejected it. Some were suspicious of us because we were helping the people.

Others misunderstood our mission and saw us as a business. Some may have wanted to manage the radio once it got running well, but they wanted to manage it in a different way. Jealousy is hard to avoid. But this happens in life. We shouldn't be surprised. I take comfort in a couple of common sayings: "There is a bit of everything in the Lord's vineyard." "In the world, we see it all." There are always many opinions.

Despite the problems that were developing—things I will describe later, regarding the worst years of repression in the 1980s—we did not run away. That's the proof of our deepest commitment. That's what shows it was not merely a business for us.

In fact, we started working more than ever in 1984 and 1985, starting with a center for "precious children," as we call them. Why do we call them "precious children"? Because they are children who have special needs. They have a bad eye, or they are blind, or they have a bad hand. We don't mean "crippled," but we mean that they are precious to us. A child or an elder cannot walk. We were able to accommodate 25 children, plus 15 who lived at home and couldn't get to our center. How were we going to help them? We secured a nurse and a teacher.

# CHAPTER 6

# The dignity of the Maya

AMONG THE MAYA, BEFORE the arrival of the Spaniards, property was communal, although everyone had their own pieces of land to cultivate and provide for their children, based on the decision of the community. According to existing documents, in pre-Columbian times, the Tz'utujil lived on the northwestern, western, and southern shores of Lake Atitlán, and their lands extended toward the coast, almost to the sea. But since the arrival of the Spaniards, the governments have divided the land and set boundaries, so that each municipality controls its territory, rather than the traditional Maya villages. The dominant class has thus been able to build their plantations, planting bananas, cotton, coffee, and other products to export to the United States and other countries. In other words, they have used the land for other purposes.

## TREATED LIKE ANIMALS

Our grandparents and great-grandparents have told us how the Tz'utujil lived in ancient times. To trade with each other, they used cacao as money to buy things to eat. They also used a barter system: "I have corn. You give me beans. Others trade with coffee." This is how they exchanged goods.

Our ancestors lived without dividing up the land. There was no problem, because the land belonged to everyone in common. This practice still exists today in our communal lands. If a person has no land, he can request two or three acres from the municipality. He pays a small amount of municipal tax. This is how land management used to work. There was no one to bother us. But when the Spaniards arrived, their authorities set land boundaries.

The Spaniards thought we didn't understand anything. They thought we had no religion. They thought we had no civilization, no authorities who could dialogue. But they were wrong. The ancient Maya had their way of governing themselves. They had leaders. But the Spaniards did not recognize our ability to work together. When they arrived, they took over the reins of government.

I have to call this a forceful domination, an invasion, rather than a so-called "discovery." To discover a thing is to talk, to communicate, to say, "What's up? How can we help you?" It is not to steal.

They treated us as if we didn't know anything. They treated us like animals. Why do I say this? They used our grandparents to carry their burdens like pack animals. They sold them in groups of 10 to 15 to other more powerful landowners: "Look, you want workers? Here are ten. Give me such-and-such." And the poor Tz'utujiles or other Maya would be tied up and sent into the hands of others who needed labor. This is the way they entered the continent, according to the stories of our ancestors.

I am not making all this up. Of course I have not seen directly what happened in other centuries. But you can read about it in books that tell how the Maya were sold by groups to other dominant people. Some came to sell us. Others became owners.

Where then is our dignity as people, as indigenous people, as children of God, in such a system? As children of God, what was our status? They did not treat us with dignity. They did not dialogue to see what we could do. They did not want to pay well for the value of our work, nor did they want to provide enough food for the welfare of our families.

I would invite those who are interested to read more. There are plenty of books. I recently read a big book by the bishop who fought against the mistreatment of the Maya. It was the famous Bishop Bartolomé de las Casas. He wrote to the king of Spain advocating for the indigenous people. But why did he have to ask the king of Spain to treat us well? The root of the domination was not in Guatemala, but in Spain. For 500 years we have suffered much from that legacy.

## THE *LATIFUNDISTA* SYSTEM

That is how the indigenous people have been left with smaller and smaller plots of land, which are more and more difficult to cultivate. We are not talking just about Santiago and other municipalities around Lake Atitlán, but about all the municipalities throughout Guatemala. Across the lake, San Marcos does not have much land. The same goes for San Pablo, Santa Maria, and that whole area; it is full of rocks and ravines! If you visit, you will see big, tall rocks. There is nowhere to plant. They only grow small vegetable gardens along the lakeshore. Pure stone and sandy soil.

There are many history books that talk about this treatment of the indigenous people, in which the powerful took away our lands. But this is not only a story in books. It is a story that our grandparents and our great-grandparents told us, about how we have been treated. When I was little, my grandfather told us about how the indigenous people were used to open new roads. There were no machines, no tractors, so the rulers forcibly expropriated the manual labor of indigenous people. They took them to open routes on the coast for railroads.

Indigenous people were also taken annually to the plantations on the coast to plant and harvest all kinds of products. The coast is where the land-owners control the flattest and most productive land in the country. The indigenous had to go for months at a time, leaving their families behind. Otherwise, they had to hide for a few days so they could stay here and cultivate their own small tracts of land, growing crops to support the family. The system brought a lot of suffering!

One would have liked to talk to other people on the coast, but the indigenous people did not necessarily understand each other, because they spoke different Mayan languages and did not understand Spanish. There was no one to teach them either. The foremen did not understand the laborers because they only spoke Spanish, and we spoke Tz'utujil or other Mayan languages. The authorities only knew how to communicate with signs that said, "You! Get to work!" "Open the road."

So many things were done to our ancestors. It is a painful story, the way the elders lived, something that young people of today could not imagine, even if they wanted to hear about it.

## THE PAST THAT IS STILL PRESENT

During the 1960s the economy of Santiago Atitlán slowly began to modernize. Still, the dominant class continued to subjugate us through their plantations and their work in the fields. They gave people work on the coast through contractors. They no longer took us to work by force. Instead, they took advantage of the poverty that had resulted from having taken away our land in the past.

In my youth I went to the coast to work to support the family. We found work there every year planting crops. Then, for a few months we picked cotton, coffee, and sugar cane. If someone wanted to rent a piece of land instead, one had to plant grass for the cattle and plant productive trees. This was the rent payment to the plantation owners. People who work on the coast are paid very little. It is not a fair wage, but we had to do it to survive. That is why there were many malnourished children, because a father or brother came back from the coast with so little money in his pocket.

To pick cotton, which I did in my youth, they took us almost to the seashore. It took two or three hours to get there from Santiago. The contractors took us in trucks as if we were cattle. Obviously, that was not safe. I remember two or three times when the trucks carrying people to the coast had accidents. The truck's brakes went out, and a number of people died.

Who took care of them? No one. Nobody offered help. "Let them die, let them die," was the attitude of the authorities. What could we do? People needed work and there were no organizations to protect *campesinos*. I don't remember in what year they started, but some *campesino* organizations began to form. I don't have the details in my head, but I know that they were repressed during the civil war.

The truth is this: few national leaders were interested in our welfare. In Guatemala some people dominate the country, enjoying the fruit of the land. But who speaks for us? Who is going to convince them to improve the conditions of the poor? Who stands up for us? Who even listens to us?

The development that we have witnessed, like the construction of schools, has often been funded by embassies, churches, and other NGOs (nongovernmental organizations) that are usually not from our country. In other words, those who are in key positions at the national level do not really prioritize their own people. Instead, they focus on how to send products abroad. They do big national projects, but it is for them. They make themselves the masters.

This is a bit of the history of the indigenous people in Guatemala. It is the history that we indigenous have all shared. We have spent many years with bitterness and pain. These are the pains we have lived through: looking for work, looking for something to eat, looking to buy a little corn, planting a little corn and beans. Nowadays, we also cultivate coffee, and sell products like avocados, something we didn't do in the past.

## COMMUNITY IMPACT

This whole system of contempt and exploitation of indigenous people has impacted the community in various ways. It is a source of community divisions and mutual mistreatment among us. Too often we fail to dialogue, we fail to communicate, even though we still have the same needs. We have never achieved a meeting among all the churches and denominations, for example, for the purpose of coordinating our common efforts on behalf of the people.

I spoke in the previous chapter about the need for schools and our struggle to establish more of them here in Santiago, with enough teachers so that the children could complete more grades. For poor families, it can still be difficult for their children to reach the sixth grade. And to get to high school or continue on to college? Even harder. We have plenty of motivation, but not all of us have been able to get an education. In many cases, our parents couldn't support us. They couldn't afford it. Many young people wanted to study. Many young people have the ability to study, but they have not been able to do so.

It was only possible for some to study, thanks to support from abroad. The Micatokla mission sent young people to junior high and high school, colleges, universities, and some to seminaries—but they were few. Nor did the foreigners bring dollars in a sack. No. They only had a little to help with. Besides, as foreigners they could not interfere in state administrative matters, which is supposed to be a governmental responsibility.

With the construction and the development we have achieved to date, our youth can benefit, at least to some extent. But now we have another challenge: getting the young people who receive advanced education to dedicate their abilities to the people and the poor, not just to pursuing their own interests. In this sense, we still need the message of Jesus that Father Stanley emphasized to us, to love our neighbor and dedicate ourselves to the common good.

Furthermore, the education that has been offered in Guatemala has not always been adapted to our indigenous culture and reality. While we must take advantage of every educational opportunity, this does not mean that the education available is adequate, given our challenges. I have often said how unfortunate it is that teachers and professors do not talk enough about how to live as families, as friends, in community with the people. Today the situation is improving, but not all teachers speak Tz'utujil or understand our culture. Some do, thank God. But we still need specific topics that relate to our actual lives. We should be teaching young people the skills they need to live a rich and communal life. The mismatch between the education system and our culture is another effect of the historical treatment of indigenous people.

Further still, there are many who now have their degrees, but have no work other than selling oranges in the market or ice cream on the street. There is not enough work. We need people who understand everything they learned at university and can now put it in practice: how to live, how to support themselves, how to contribute to the community. Young people need to take pride in doing their own work and not wait for someone else to solve their problems.

The historical system of exploitation is also at the root of the difficulty of supporting a family. A young person has to think, Can I support a family with children or not? Sadly, not everyone can support a family or support a child who needs to study. If we were to take a census right now, we would find only a few young people who have gone to university. I would say there are maybe 80 to 90 young people who have left Santiago to go to university elsewhere. In the university extension programs here, it could be more—perhaps 150 to 200 young people. But that's a small percentage for a town of 50,000 people. Very small. We don't have anthropologists of our own, for example. We don't have many other professions.

## MAKING IT, WITHIN THE SYSTEM

That is the treatment we have received since the coming of the Spaniards. Our ancestors were not passive, though. They took initiatives to improve their economic conditions. And now there have been changes in commerce, in agriculture, in artisanal work, and in trade. Our people always figure out a way. In Santiago, for example, many of the Tz'utujil have gone into commerce in other towns and other departments. Some have even gone to other countries. With their handicrafts and the new capacities they have developed, they have advanced.

If you look around here in town, you see many construction projects. You no longer see the Santiago of before. We have many businesspeople who live in the capital and who have supported their children well. Some have been able to help their children to receive a university education. It means that we have taken a few steps forward economically, with professionals in more areas of work.

I have also seen some indigenous people who have married *ladinos* and some *ladino* people who have married indigenous. This means that we are breaking down barriers. We are reaching a stage in which we accept each other and understand that we are equal.[1]

There are still many people in the neighborhoods, in the villages, on the farms, and in the rural areas, however, who have no work. Children continue to suffer. They have no housing. Sometimes there is no clean drinking water. I worry that we are starting to experience a new division: some are doing better, while others suffer even worse living conditions.

Another dilemma is that, to some extent, indigenous people have to adapt to the *ladino* culture in order to gain dignity and recognition in society. In other words, they must conform to the dominant culture. Perhaps not entirely, but somehow students and those who work in commerce have to understand and learn *ladino* customs in order to live better economically. Behind all this cultural and economic pressure is the force of worldwide globalization that affects all Guatemalans, both *ladino* and indigenous.

Of course, to completely abandon our culture is difficult. For example, in my culture, I won't let anyone tell me, "Stop wearing your typical pants or stop wearing that shirt; don't wear indigenous dress anymore." I simply cannot do that. I can't even go for a walk without my hat. It's the culture. Many of my fellow Tz'utujil are like that. They can't take a walk without their hats. They can't go to work without eating a few tortillas at every meal.

1. In Guatemala, the term *ladino* means a person of non-Maya or Hispanic culture. It does not necessarily correspond to the ethnic descent of the person. Someone of indigenous descent can become *ladino* if he or she leaves the indigenous culture behind. In Guatemala, the term does not indicate a Jewish identity or background, as in other Latin American countries and in Spain. For detailed studies, see Richard N. Adams, *Cultural Surveys of Panama—Nicaragua—El Salvador—Honduras*, Scientific Publications No. 33 (Washington, DC: Pan American Sanitary Bureau of the World Health Association, 1957), 267–70; and Severo Martínez Peláez, "The Ladino," in *The Guatemala Reader: History, Culture, Politics*, ed. Greg Grandin, Deborah Levenson, and Elizabeth Oglesby, The Latin America Readers (Durham, NC: Duke University Press, 2011), 129–32.

Moreover, the domination we face now is not so much at the national level. It is at the international level. Why do I say that? Well, many people have cell phones and cable TV by now. Many people stop wearing indigenous clothing and buy used clothes imported by the bale—foreign clothes. But you have to see why. A pair of imported used pants costs three to five quetzals, while a traditional pair of pants like mine, made from fabric that is woven on a loom and hand embroidered, costs from 800 to 1500 quetzals, or even more. The same for the lovely *huipils* for women. The global powers have dominated our cultures.

Another sign of domination is visible in the garbage all over the streets. When I was a kid, we didn't have a lot of technology, but we didn't have a lot of garbage either. We only had canoes to get across the lake back then. There were no motorboats. To transport people to other municipalities living on the shore of Lake Atitlán, they used big canoes, with lots of people rowing, including the passengers themselves. There was very little garbage back then—no nylon, no plastics, so many things that exist now. We ate only locally grown food from the countryside. We brought it, prepared it at home, and ate. No canned food. We were totally unaware of these things, until around 1965. Fertilizer came, insecticides came, and a lot of other things came—including nylon, plastics, plastic shoes, synthetic shirts, processed foods.

Where did that garbage come from? It's from commerce. It comes with domination by global powers. We get cell phones and a lot of other things. But there is already so much that we can't control the cleanup. The plastic reaches the sea. All part of globalization. It means that to survive in this world, we have to study hard to figure out how to proceed. It may be that globalization brings us some good and healthy things. But many people also understand that because of it, there are killings, there are robberies, there is repression.

We must also recognize the phenomena by which we harm ourselves. Some do not want to work. Before God, that is also a sin. Some of us do not want to support a family; we just want to hang out. We tell ourselves, "I am free." But what freedom? Just hanging out without working does not make for much of a life. What about your child? What about your wife? Or your mother and father? Perhaps they are already aging and need your help.

Undoubtedly, our parents and our grandparents found opportunities to enjoy themselves in times gone by. They had their customs. They participated in the village celebrations during the holidays. But it was not a matter of staying out every day without working. No. Everything has its time—to be able to walk, to visit friends, to meet friends, to enjoy time with them, to go to church, to listen more to the word of God.

## THE DIGNITY OF THE GOSPEL

Looking back, I realize how many things began to change in the mid-1960s—in the economy, with technology, nationally and also internationally. It was supposedly the Decade of Development worldwide, as declared by the United Nations. It may be that this context provided one of the reasons for the Micatokla mission to start its work. More missions from other churches and nongovernmental organizations also came here. What is certain is that the changes we experienced the most were evident in the parish itself, with the arrival of the Micatokla team and the missionary priests.

They did a good job. The missionaries who came knew why, and how. They first studied the history of our peoples, the life of the Maya and their history. They understood where we came from and how to work. They arrived with a spirit of brother- and sisterhood toward the community, not with criticism of our culture or religion. Quite the opposite. They asked us, "How can we help you?"

I believe that Father Stanley's identification with the community was made possible because he had already come well trained. A feeling for other human beings had been born in him, and it blossomed here in Guatemala. He did not come just for fun, but to carry out a task and fulfil a mission. He was ready to give himself to humanity. Giving of himself as he did, while finding himself in such a needy and exploited society that faced so many problems, he brought a spirit that was born of love for others. Having taken a step to become a priest, he had more than ideas in his head. God had also touched his heart. I believe that he wept for the people in the sufferings they were going through, because every day he saw the problems of the children and of the elderly. People could feel his brotherly warmth, how much he cared for them, how much he loved them.

This identification was the best way to help people. He could not go to protest openly on the plantations, but in his homilies he insisted that no one was to dominate another person. Everyone is a child of God. What he could do was preach that we need to be treated with equality, out of love—treated as children of God. He called on us to fulfill the word of God.

It can be hard to get through someone's head and tell them what to do. But his message of what we should do in our life did get into our hearts.

That's why he never wanted to abandon the people. He said, "I am not going to leave town. I am going to continue working." Many of his colleagues left us and went back to their own land. He alone stayed, because he felt he had made a sacred commitment to the community—like a marriage—to learn all its characteristics, its culture, and to stay true.

That was the reason why he searched for ways to improve relationships (*buscando la convivencia*) with the *cofrades*. After all, how would they feel if they were rejected by the church? For that reason, he sought to grow closer to them. He told them, "Don't be ashamed. Come. Attend the church's meetings." He approached them and other people so that everyone would understand each other, and he could understand what they wanted. Father Stanley came with a model of evangelization that allowed him to better explain the message of Christ to them.

They in turn explained their way of celebrating. Thus a dialogue developed. As their cooperative, respectful relationship grew, they gave him the symbol of the *cofradía*, the *xq'ajk'oj*, a cloth that the *cofradía* use, that they hung around his neck. He treasured it deeply, wearing it when he celebrated mass. He continued to walk around wearing it until he died. It is another sign that he had entered deeply into the culture of the people.

Many people misunderstood Father Stanley because he did not reject other religions or denominations. I clearly remember an incident with some of those Americans who wear white shirts—the Mormons. Three of their young men went on a hike to the volcano and got lost in the mountains. Father Stanley said, "I'm going to take some people to go look for them." He never said he didn't care about people because they were of another religion. No. He helped young people from other churches. I was impressed.

He never turned anyone away. Just because someone contradicts my religion, do they have to stay outside? No. If someone needed help for sports, or to celebrate a small party in one of the *cofradías*, or even a loudspeaker for the Evangelicals—he helped them! Because what he wanted was to gain the trust of the people, so that we could live more truly (*convivir*) as sisters and brothers. If a group of *campesinos* came asking for support, he would look for a way to help. The parish helped the poor get a place to live and build their houses.

For me, he was a great priest. He showed us how to work. And this had a great effect on the people. Many admired him. Among the people in town nobody spoke against the priest. The people grew closer in order to understand each other, to serve each other more. He taught us how we should live together with our neighbors. That is why he always said not to fight, not to hate, because everything is love, and we need to practice it. People admired his work, along with his reflections in his homilies.

At the same time, Father Stanley trusted us too. The radio station was an idea that the missionaries came up with, but in a few years, they turned it over to the community. The parish built a hospital for the same purpose, the "Hospitalito" that they eventually gave to the community and that continues to this day. Unfortunately, when a landslide came down the volcano during Hurricane Stan in 2005, the hospital had to change its location. But again, it got rebuilt with the support of the dioceses of Oklahoma.

Thank God that some of the Guatemalan priests and nuns who have come to serve since Micatokla left have also sought to live closely with us, speaking with us and giving their homilies in Mayan languages, for example. But unfortunately not all of them. We have had priests who are fellow Guatemalans, of indigenous descent, who want to speak only in Spanish. They are Kakchiquel, and between the Tz'utujil and the Kakchiquel we can understand each other. However, they no longer communicate with us in an indigenous language. They say, "I am not Atiteco, and I cannot speak Tz'utujil." Why? They can speak in Kakchiquel if they want to. We will listen to them. We will understand them. "But I can't," they say. "I didn't study it in the seminary. They spoke Spanish to me, and now I have learned a lot of Spanish."

I would like to ask: Who controls your spirituality, your commitment? Padre Apla's had to struggle to speak in Tz'utujil. But for that reason, he himself commissioned the translation of the New Testament and the prayers into Tz'utujil. He came from Oklahoma and he learned. There is comparatively little difference between Tz'utujil and Kakchiquel, very little! Why don't the bishops insist that, before transferring to serve here, new priests learn Tz'utujil? That would be my recommendation.

Of the many projects that Micatokla launched in the parish, only some continue. The administration of the school continues, but the hospital became an independent entity. Of course, personal and family assistance from the parish continues for the needy. Nonetheless, there is no longer as much interest in doing major initiatives as Father Stanley and the rest of the Micatokla team did. Perhaps this is because there is no longer as much staff. Still, sometimes I worry that some parts of the Church in Guatemala and in Latin America are losing their commitment to social action. I am encouraged, though, that Pope Francis has insisted that pastors, bishops, and missionaries continue to project an integral, wholistic evangelization, which includes the social. All of us as Christians must collaborate with the Church in this integral evangelization.

# CHAPTER 7

# Padre Apla's and Maya spirituality

WE HAVE ALREADY SEEN that Father Stanley was a priest and a Christian who sought unity and the common good within the whole community. That is why he opened his hand of collaboration with everyone, whether or not they were Catholics who participated in the life of the parish. He sought reconciliation. But that was still a very difficult challenge for him. Because our religious situation here in Atitlán is very complicated.[1]

It has been complicated since the arrival of the Spanish. And during the decades of the last century it has become more and more complicated. We have divisions between Catholics, between Evangelicals, between Catholics and Evangelicals, and between those who try to maintain Maya practices. Whoever seeks reconciliation can be suspect from all sides. When I feel this kind of suspicion myself, I take courage from the example of Father Stanley, Padre Apla's. He found ways to improve our communal and religious relations, to some extent, for a while. But he also drew criticism. And if they criticized even him, what else can we expect from others? We should follow his example.

1. For a recent ethnographic study of the religious situation in Santiago Atitlán that coincides with Juan Ajtzip's account in this chapter and offers further details, see Jakob Egeris Thorsen, "Modern and Orthodox—the Transformation of Christianity in Atitlán and the Marginalization of Maya Traditionalism," in *"What Is Human?" Theological Encounters with Anthropology* (Göttingen; Bristol, CT: Vandenhoeck & Ruprecht, 2016), 403–30.

## THE COMPLEX LEGACY OF THE SPANIARDS' FAITH

When the Spanish came, the Maya had their own religion. At first, they did not want to mix with the Spanish religion. They didn't want to go near the mass. The Spaniards were looking to evangelize and began to think about what they could do to attract the Maya to their masses and celebrations. Still, since very few villages had parishes yet; the priests came only once in a while.

That is why the first Catholic missionaries from Europe looked for a way to appeal to the Maya. According to what we know from history, they organized events with Mexican-style dances and invited the people to come and watch. That is how they gained the trust of the people: they invited them to participate in and learn the dances. They used this type of festive event to celebrate the patron saints. Then at some point the Spaniards stopped the dancing and started the celebration of the mass. This is how they managed to attract the interest of the people, so that they would come in to hear what the Catholic faith was all about.

Nonetheless, even though the Spaniards founded parishes on the strength of the participation of the Maya themselves, and built churches, they did not keep enough priests to shepherd everyone. This is where the historical *cofradías* originated. They were founded by the Spaniards themselves, to care for and maintain the saints—the statues of the saints that they had placed inside the church.

Later, after the Spanish missionaries and pastors departed, and following some strong earthquakes in the eighteenth century, everything fell apart. The people themselves were not trained to evangelize or teach, and that is why the parish almost fell apart, as I understand it. After one of the strong earthquakes, the roof and the domes of the church fell down. They had to take the saints out to people's houses. They organized themselves in the form of *cofradías* and began to have more meetings with the people in the various neighborhoods. In the following decades, when there was no one to support the church, the *cofradías* were the ones who maintained the church, according to the histories that have come down to us.

The historical *cofradías* struggled to maintain the church. They struggled to rebuild the church, with minimal supervision from the Spaniards. While they cared for the saints, they also began to take care of the church, since there was no one else to do that. They worked that way for many years, because there was no resident priest in the parish. I don't know if they understood Catholic doctrine very well, but they deserve credit for their efforts over so many years.

During the 1930s and 1940s, Spanish missionaries began to minister to the population on a more regular basis, although we still did not have resident pastors. To spread awareness of the faith and improve the formation of the faithful, they began to train lay catechists and promoted Catholic Action. They worked among the youth in those times. There was already a little more of a relationship between the people and the priests, with more services and meetings to teach Catholic doctrine. Responsibility for taking care of the church was passed to the catechists and Catholic Action. They also formed a Pro-Reconstruction Committee for the church.

I don't know if the intent was to isolate the *cofradías*, but that was one of the results. More conflicts grew. The *cofrades* felt rejected. They devoted themselves less to the Catholic faith and parish activities, and more to their own rites, which seem to be a mixture of Catholic rites, Maya rites, and their own innovations.

Then, when the Micatokla mission came, the North American missionaries looked for a way to improve pastoral care for these people from the *cofradías*. No one was ministering to them, after all. The catechists were not going to work in this field. The *cofradías* were isolated. Father Stanley saw that they were working on their own, and he approached them, seeking to draw them into a closer relationship to the parish. For him, this was a way of evangelizing. They still had their own ways and customs for how to celebrate in church. For example, they had their own way of celebrating Holy Week, and they still do. In order not to find himself in conflict with them, Father Stanley tried to coordinate activities with them, and at times correct some of their practices.

## THE COMPLEX HERITAGE OF THE MAYA

When visitors arrive at the Santiago dock by boat, a guide will undoubtedly offer to take them to visit a character called Maximón (in Tz'utujil, *Maxmoon k'aam*), staying at the house of a *cofrade*. Supposedly, Maximón is a Maya figure, and that is why he attracts so much attention from tourists. Some anthropologists claim that he plays a role in the Maya cosmovision or worldview by resisting Spanish domination. But therein lies the doubt that some of us have, and the reason why not everyone believes in him here in town. Although he may possibly represent this resistance now, there is no evidence that Maximón existed before the Spanish conquest. I don't know what year Maximón was born, but according to the stories, it was when the church and the municipality were already in place. So it is difficult to conclude that he represents the spirituality of the ancient Maya per se.[2]

The most authentic Maya practices are not so easily encountered by a visitor. For centuries, the Spanish discouraged and even repressed them. Now this is no longer the case, and there are those who call themselves Maya priests, who offer to do their prayers in public, but among the Maya people there is still reserve. As I recounted in chapter 4 concerning my grandfather, the most authentic Maya celebrations are practiced within the family. They are not at all a show for the public, but something between a Maya practitioner and the Supreme Being, showing gratitude to the owner of the world for their crops, their families, and all the nature that God has given us. They go to do their prayers on the mountaintop or in a secret cave. These are places where the Maya make their petitions to God. They do that, and no one can stop them. Nobody forbids it, nor is it seen in public.

In this way some Maya customs continue, among the people who really know how to say their prayers, and do not depend on the *cofradías*. Those who really have the heart of gratitude to the Supreme Being know how to do Maya prayers. They do it in the field or in some place that is sacred to the Maya. That is where they use candles, incense, flowers, and other things.

To be sure, there are differences among the Tz'utujil people, even among those who try to maintain Maya religious traditions—what we call *costumbre* or "the custom." There are not only differences between Catholics and Evangelicals, for example. The *cofradías* still insist on caring for the saints. But the people's opinion of them has long been mixed. In their meetings, they like to have a few drinks. The young Catholics have not looked well on them, at least since the time when the catechists got started in the 1930s and 1940s, given their influence among the Catholic faithful. That is

2. For exhaustive studies of Maximón and the role he plays in Tz'utujil culture, see Vincent James Stanzione, *Rituals of Sacrifice: Walking the Face of the Earth on the Sacred Path of the Sun: A Journey through the Tz'utujil Maya World of Santiago Atitlán*, photography by Paul Harbaugh, illus. Angelika Bauer (Albuquerque: University of New Mexico Press, 2003); Vincent James Stanzione and Angelika Bauer, *Los Nawales, the Ancient Ones: Merchants, Wives, and Lovers: The Creation Story of MaXimón* (Guatemala: Editorial Serviprensa S.A., 2016); and Manlio Soto Paiz, *Maximón y lo inconsciente colectivo: arquetipos y simbología* (2018). Much information on the figure of Maximón in the context of the *cofradía* worldview is also found in Robert S. Carlsen, *The War for the Heart and Soul of a Highland Maya Town*, rev. ed. (Austin: University of Texas Press, 2011).

why a separation developed. There are practitioners of *costumbre* who do not want to participate in the celebrations of the *cofradías* any more than anyone else. Or sometimes they go to the *cofradía*, but there are many more who go to hidden sacred Maya places.

Maximón continues to be a divisive figure in the community, to this day. Each *cofradía* celebrates the feast of a particular saint they have in their neighborhood. This does not present much of a problem most of the time. But during Holy Week, the *cofradias* insist on putting up a tiny chapel for Maximón on one side of the churchyard. At times there are clashes when people go to follow the Good Friday procession. These are not usually violent clashes, but there have been tensions.

## PADRE APLA'S'S RECEPTIVITY

Within the context of the Maya culture, Father Stanley wanted to get to know, communicate with, and relate to the people of the *cofradía* from the moment he arrived. With his attitude of reconciliation, he sought ways to coexist (*convivir*) with them. He invited them to participate in the mass, to hear the word of God, and to better understand Christian doctrine. He invited them to receive the sacrament of marriage and all that the Church asks of the faithful. And some of them did. Father Stanley's participation with the *cofradía* was a way to gain their trust. To be present with them meant living and working together (*convivir*), not only in the feasts for patron saints, but also on Sundays. Father Stanley did his biblical readings and his reflections with this in mind.[3]

3. This attitude is in conformity with the teaching of the Second Vatican Council regarding other religions and the respect that missionaries and priests should show. The declaration *Nostra Aetate* affirms that, although incomplete, non-Christian religions carry truth and goodness within them, for the other religions in the world strive to respond in various ways to the restlessness of the human heart, proposing paths of life, by way of their doctrines, norms of life, and sacred rites:

> The Catholic Church rejects nothing of what is true and holy in these religions. It has a high regard for the manner of life and conduct, the precepts and doctrines which, although differing in many ways from its own teaching, nevertheless often reflect a ray of that truth which enlightens all men and women. Yet it proclaims and is in duty bound to proclaim without fail, Christ who is the way, the truth and the life (Jn 14:6). In him, in whom God reconciled all things to himself (see 2 Cor 5:18–19), people find the fullness of their religious life.
>
> The church, therefore, urges its sons and daughters to enter with prudence and charity into discussion and collaboration with members of other religions. Let Christians, while witnessing to their own faith and way of life, acknowledge, preserve and encourage the

I think Father Stanley began by studying the attitude of the *cofradías* here in Santiago and the attitude of the Catholic Church, especially within Catholic Action. He saw the existing divisions. He learned about the role that the *cofradías* had played in the past. Then he approached them. For a long time, the *cofradías* had been holding their meetings every week or two in front of the church or in the corridor of the church. He began to join them there. He would sit with them for a while. He would discuss the problems in each *cofradía*, the needs they had, and the way they were working. He would offer to help them, always inviting them to the church so that every Sunday they could participate.[4]

---

spiritual and moral truths found among non-Christians, together with their social life and culture.

To promote this kind of rapprochement, the Second Vatican Council's declaration on the missionary work of the Church, *Ad Gentes*, insists that Catholic missionaries prepare themselves "so that they might have a general knowledge of peoples, cultures and religions, not only with regard to the past but also with respect to the present time." For "Whoever is to go among another people must hold their inheritance, language and way of life in high esteem." Likewise, the preparation of local priests should not alienate them from their cultures:

> [The] general requirements for priestly training, both pastoral and practical, which have been laid down by the council, must be accompanied with a willingness to come to grips with the particular nation's own way of thinking and acting. Therefore, the minds of the students must be opened and refined so that they will better understand and appreciate the culture of their own people; in philosophy and theology they should examine the relationship between the traditions and religion of their homeland and Christianity. In the same way, priestly formation must take account of the pastoral needs of the region; the students must learn the history, goal and method of missionary activity, as well as the particular social, economic and cultural conditions of their own people. They should be formed in the spirit of ecumenism and properly prepared for friendly dialogue with non-Christians. All this demands that, as far as possible, their studies for the priesthood should be undertaken in close contact with the way of life of their own people.

(All documents from the Second Vatican Council are available at https://www.vatican.va/archive/hist_councils/ii_vatican_council/index.htm, or in the updated English translation quoted here: Austin Flannery, OP, general editor, *Vatican Council II: Constitutions, Decrees, Declarations: The Basic Sixteen Documents*, A completely revised translation in inclusive language [Collegeville, MN: Liturgical Press, 2014].)

4. In her biography of Rother, María Ruiz Scaperlanda confirms this attitude of his towards the confraternities and their practices:

> By all accounts, Stanley was intrigued by the *cofradía* and its traditions, and he seemed to see it as an ingenious attempt to hold connections to their Mayan past. But above all, Stanley appeared interested in making sure that the Tz'utujil did not consider their Mayan roots and connections as evil, wanting to purify and incorporate what was good in the *cofradía* traditions and practices into orthodox Catholicism. Insofar as his conscience would allow, Stanley cooperated with the *cofradía* and befriended their individual members.

Sometimes he was criticized by the Catholic community and by the Evangelical churches for visiting the *cofradías*. So he limited his visits, but he did not stop interacting with them. He did not continue visiting the *cofradías* in each neighborhood, but he continued to sit down with them in front of the church. He listened to them. He did not go every day. He did not go every week. But he was looking for relationships with these people. Father Stanley also always wanted to catechize the *cofradías*.

That is why the *cofradías* agreed to make some changes inside the church, when the parish made repairs to the altar and changed the location of the saints. In February 1976 there was a very hard earthquake in Guatemala, in which many died. The earthquake hit us here in Santiago, but there was not as much damage as in other parts of the country. However, it was also an opportunity to unite as a community. The *cofradías* and Catholic Action formed a committee to repair and rebuild the church. That was everyone's job. They researched what the church needed, what manual labor the town could provide, and what donations were needed. Through the radio we asked for help from the towns that did not suffer so much, and we coordinated the distribution of money, corn, beans, food, and other supplies for the suffering communities. We were able to offer a lot to people in other areas.

The committee, Catholic Action, and the *cofradía* really worked well together. I was there collaborating with them, and my father was also a member of the committee. They invited me to be secretary of the committee. I personally experienced the life of the committee in its meetings with the *cofradías* and Padre Apla's. We worked together cooperatively. I saw it and better understood the way he related to the people.

## REPAIRING THE ALTAR

Perhaps the best example of Father Stanley's receptive attitude towards the Maya cosmovision is the initiative he took in repairing the large altar on the wall at the back of the church. It is very old, made of wood. It is thought to have been built as early as the sixteenth century, when the church itself was built. It combines figures and motifs of both the Maya and the Catholic faith. But because of so many years and the humidity we have here in Atitlán, its condition deteriorated, and during a previous earthquake it suffered serious damage.

See Scaperlanda, *The Shepherd Who Didn't Run: Father Stanley Rother, Martyr from Oklahoma* (Huntington, IN: Our Sunday Visitor, 2015), 115.

The ancient altar at Santiago Apóstol Parish, Santiago Atitlán, repaired by commission under the direction of Blessed Father Rother in the 1970s, integrating Maya and Roman Catholic iconography. (Photo by Deacon John Donaghy.)

The severe earthquake of 1976 caused even more damage, and that prompted Father Stanley to initiate a complete rebuilding of the altar. No one had repaired the altars for many centuries until the missionaries from Oklahoma came. Father Stanley liked the old altar very much. He himself worked on its reconstruction. He hired two brothers who were sculptors to repair it. They were brothers who had been trained in sculpture by a nun from the Micatokla team. The altar was rebuilt by the people from here who repaired it with their labor, informed by our culture. It was a very excellent restoration.[5]

## THE RELIGIOUS SITUATION IN SANTIAGO TODAY

Today, Evangelical churches have multiplied, with their various names, leaders, and beliefs. As Catholics, we have never found a path of dialogue with their pastors. This has further complicated relations between the various Catholic factions here. To deflect criticism from the Evangelicals, some Catholics try to prove that we are 100 percent Catholic Christian, leaving behind every Maya custom. That is why many are afraid to study and discover the good things we inherited from our Maya ancestors.

The clashes result because at times we just do not understand each other. Like Padre Apla's, I believe that the *cofradías* could play a positive role in the parish. Unfortunately, they lose their credibility when they do not receive the sacraments or learn Church teaching. In addition, they themselves compete with each other to attract tourists, because that allows them to demand donations from those who want to observe their rites and take pictures of Maximón. It is fine for them to have their own devotionals to honor the saints they care for, and to have their processions in some way. But we all have to seek mutual understanding.

The activities of the *cofradías* continue to this day, especially in the processions during the feast of Santiago [St. James] the Apostle, the patron saint of the town, and on the Fridays of Lent and Holy Week. They start from the corridor in front of the church and process four blocks around the church and central park. On the Fridays of Lent, there is the procession of the Lord Jesus carrying the cross, and then on Good Friday, the procession of Our Lord Entombed. On each block, one of the *cofradías* is in charge of setting up a small altar with various saints. When I was a child, there was a small chapel on each corner, but over time the practice was lost, and now there is no longer even one. People took over the spaces as they built houses and commercial stores. All processions are accompanied by band music. In the past, a small group of ladies used to throw flowers to the saints as well. To this day, the processions are accompanied by songs of praise made by the *cofradía* elders.

5. For a detailed study of the altar and its iconography, both Catholic and Maya, see Allen J. Christenson, *Art and Society in a Highland Maya Community: The Altarpiece of Santiago Atitlán* (Austin: University of Texas Press, 2001).

On Good Friday the procession is the largest. It is accompanied by the people, carrying large candles and incense. In the streets, young people organize and prepare carpets (*alfombras*) of beautiful figures made from colored sawdust. They also create wooden arches across the streets, hanging fruit, and animal decorations. Maximón spends three days in a small chapel in the corner of the church square during Holy Week, and then on Good Friday he comes out to cut into the line of the procession, placing himself behind Our Lord Entombed. Maximón's procession follows behind everything for an hour. He walks to the stone cross that is in the middle of the plaza, and then afterwhile he breaks from the procession and goes to the house of the *cofradía* where he's staying, accompanied by their members, along with his own band music. Here every year we see both the collaboration that exists and the spiritual competition that the Atiteco people experience, leaving us with divisions.

These practices continue, although now with more competition than coordination. When the parish moves its official church services out onto the plaza on Holy Thursday, the *cofradías* take up spaces inside the church with their own prayers, brass bands, and heavy wooden floats. Good Friday then brings competing processions, winding their ways through town. But here is where we have to mention the Evangelicals again, who have been gaining strength since the 1950s. They have criticized not only the *cofradías* but also the Catholic saints, calling them idols. I think this was one of the reasons why the catechists and those of Catholic Action have tried so hard to distinguish themselves even more from the *cofradías*.

## CONCLUDING ANALYSIS

I still wonder sometimes how best to characterize the faith of our people, divided as we are in so many ways. Padre Apla's was looking for collaboration and even reconciliation. But many others remain judgmental. They criticize, saying that these are the real Catholics, that this is real Catholicism, and others do not count. Certainly we do not all think exactly the same. The *cofradías* are one thing, and the Catholic faith is distinct. Who can say? I have no idea right now whether all the *cofrades* would call themselves Catholic or not. If they are Catholic, they would have to comply with the regulations of being Catholic. But if an Atiteco wants to be a *cofrade*, he or she should think hard about what goes on, how they practice, what they do.

For my part I would consider them Catholics, but with other thoughts on how to celebrate in their *cofradía* with their marimbas, guitars, and other instruments. That's fine. I still find it strange that we are so divided in this way, between Evangelicals, *cofradías*, Catholics, and all. In 1990, when there was the strong clash between the soldiers and the people of Santiago, the whole population was able to come together—all of them! It no longer mattered that one was from the *cofradía* and another from the Evangelicals and who knows what else. It makes me wonder why we cannot simply follow Father Stanley's example of collaboration and reconciliation. Do we always need the provocation of a crisis, when we already have the word of God indicating the way forward?

I will say this much: In spite of certain tensions, the good thing that can be observed is that all the people have a Christian faith to honor God, who has given us life. This is what our ancestors taught us, and there is reason to say, "We have the courage to respect the different streams of the Church and thus to each give the glory to the one God, the Supreme Being, with his son Jesus Christ."

# CHAPTER 8

# The repression

THE REPRESSION THAT THE community experienced during the 1980s is a sad story. Until the late 1970s, we had not experienced any such problems. We knew some of the news of the civil war in Guatemala, but it had not touched our region. The local authorities collaborated with social action projects and were in favor of the cooperatives, because they saw what they contributed to economic progress in the community. We were looking for work, wanting to improve life for our children. We made efforts, even though it was tough. Therefore, it was a great surprise and shock when violence suddenly increased here.

## A GROWING CRISIS

In those days, jobs didn't pay well, either on the farms or in the community. There was not much land to cultivate any more. Seeing the suffering families, young people began to look for ways, both local and national, to improve the conditions of inequality that we suffered. When the army began to close down the nonviolent paths to social change, yes, the guerrillas entered town. As they had done in other communities throughout Guatemala, the guerrillas briefly entered in June 1980, and the young people heard their critique of the government. But I'm getting ahead of the story. The work of the church here was always in favor of projects that promoted the Christian faith and the common good of society by nonviolent means.

Already in the mid-1970s here in Santiago Atitlán, we had achieved a better era, because of the work we were carrying out in the community. We always collaborated with our local communities in development, through cooperatives and committees, making improvements with literacy centers, the radio, and most of all in the parishes, because the priests and the missions were responding to more needs every day.

Of course, we wouldn't claim that these projects managed to meet all the needs in the community. It is difficult to attend to everyone, and resources are always scarce. But more needs were being met than before, and people were living better lives, thanks to both their crops and their handicrafts. In the community you did not see people fighting. You didn't see people clashing with each other. You could sleep on the shore of the lake in a canoe if you wanted, and nothing happened to you. There was no violence at all. Of course, we all still lived with economic challenges, but daily life was calm for people. People went to the countryside. They could harvest their peaches, their avocadoes, their corn. Everything was quiet. They could bring firewood, hiking either near or far. People could bring their *pacaya* (clusters of palm flowers) from the mountains near the southern plantations.

Then in the early 1980s the army came here and built a military base just outside of Santiago. They were suspicious of our development efforts. They seemed to think that if the people could organize to improve their lives, they could also organize to stand up against the injustices we suffered as *campesinos* and as Maya. Although our agricultural cooperative was encouraged by the church, the military labeled it as communist. When they repressed community development projects that were completely nonviolent, their repression caused divisions about how to respond.

In those years, guerrillas had begun to organize more at the national level. The guerrillas entered Santiago in June 1980. I remember that it was around ten o'clock at night. They came to hold a rally in the park, make some noise, get everyone's attention, and make some speeches. But not everyone woke up. The town is big, after all. Still, those who were in the park listened to their speeches. The guerrillas wanted to broadcast some announcements on the radio, but we couldn't give them access. The radio starts at five o'clock in the morning and ends at ten o'clock at night. After that, there is no more programming. The station had already been turned off when they came and asked us to broadcast; we said we couldn't. The security guard had already gone home and lived far away. We could not open up for them if we wanted.

That was in June. In mid-October of the same year, the army arrived and set up a military base in Panabaj, a kilometer away. That was the beginning of our problems in the 1980s, and things got worse quickly. The military began to investigate antigovernment and communist activities, or so they claimed. What actually happened is that, within the town itself, some people took advantage of the opportunity to accuse their enemies. People who had to go to work outside of town sometimes got caught and were accused of going to the mountains to support the guerrillas. Soon people were showing up dead, with their throats slit. Others were kidnapped, and nobody knew exactly who the culprits were.

After that, almost everyone lived in fear. They got very scared. There were a few who thought the situation was good, because the military said that they were here to take care of the people. But we said, how are they taking care of the people if no one has been bothering us? Still, the people had to accept that they would stay. At first, things were calm. However, it wasn't long before the military began to register people and accuse them of harboring clandestine groups. If someone went to the countryside, they said that they were taking food to the people in the mountains—that is, the guerrillas—and that they were collaborating. So that's how the clash began. People got very scared.

After that, our suffering began to increase, especially in terms of fear. It caused divisions within the community. Some complained to the army about others, making matters worse. People started to get upset. Everybody was afraid. Some were accused. Some were kidnapped. The military was especially suspicious of young people.

Because of this, many people mobilized in search of safety and protection, and a lot of them went to find sanctuary in the church. Whole families went to sleep there. They surprised Father Stanley with their requests to use the church as a sanctuary, but he authorized it. He comforted them, saying that they had nothing to be ashamed of, that it was okay. Many went there, while others took refuge in other neighborhoods. In other words, they looked for places where they could group together. Each family struggled with where and how to show solidarity with each other. It was a season of shock and fright.

The situation became more and more dangerous for Father Stanley as well. He saw that many people were looking for a place to stay, looking for shelters and refuge. He had sheltered some young people who were being persecuted. He sometimes had to tell them, "Sleep here under the table, because we have no more room." However, some young people were nabbed right in front of the church. They were captured and taken away.

In the midst of this situation, Father Stanley did what he could to advocate for the people. In meetings where he participated with authorities and representatives of churches or other social organizations, he insisted, "I have been living in Santiago Atitlán for 13 years. I am a missionary priest. I came from the state of Oklahoma in the United States, with the sole motive of giving testimony to Jesus Christ and showing his love for the Tz'utujil people. I had never seen any kidnappings, killings, or any of these other abuses until the army came. I had not seen anything. The people have been calm. We didn't know anything at all about masked men going around town carrying weapons. It is only now that we are seeing a lot of bad things."[1]

I recognize that some folks in town were upset that Padre Apla's was advocating for the people. That was the only meeting to which the authorities invited him, as far as I know. We could no longer achieve anything in meetings like that, given the growing problems and clashes. But Father Stanley continued to help people, even young people who wanted to take refuge. I think that's why the military authorities didn't like him, because he gave refuge to those they suspected.

That's where Father Stanley got even more involved. He said no—that we should not kill, that we should not kidnap, that no one has the right to take the life of another, that life is not something that can be bought. He insisted that life belongs to God, the One who has given us life, and we were not to kill, not to hassle each other, not to harm others, women, children, young people, or the elderly. That's how Father Stanley began to speak up to denounce the situation more and more. He heated up, really taking seriously the words of God, telling us what it means to do right and to do wrong. That is how Padre Apla's became more and more public with his prophetic criticism.

## PERSECUTION OF THE RADIO STATION

The entry of the army in October 1980 had an almost immediate impact on the radio station. On October 24th the director and some other associates of the radio station were kidnapped. Previously, I had been the director, but due to a health issue I had to withdraw. If I had still been director that year,

---

1. An account of this town hall meeting appears in Scaperlanda, *The Shepherd Who Didn't Run*, 175–77.

maybe I would have been killed. The director who replaced me had been a seminarian in Sololá and did his diaconate here in Santiago with Father Stanley. He was taken from his home and was never seen again. He had been at the radio station for only ten months, which was from January to October. His body has never been found.

I had gotten sick in July 1979. The doctor told me that I had a liver disease. He said that it was probably because of the stress of directing an institution that was respected for its work, but we were constructing our building while managing centers to train new broadcasters and working with other organizations and with young people. The doctor told me that I could continue in that position if I wanted, but that I had to slow down. So in December of 1979 I told my colleagues, "I no longer want to be director. You can appoint someone. I can no longer continue." They accepted, although they did not want to, but they had to accept, because otherwise I would get sicker.

They elected another person to replace me. The colleague they put in charge was Gaspar Culán Yataz, the former seminarian. In January he began to function as director, and in October he was kidnapped. We were all frightened. Other colleagues were also kidnapped. After Gaspar's kidnapping, three of our companions were kidnapped in a handicraft store in Antigua, Guatemala. As a consequence of all that had happened, the literacy workers in other municipalities were frightened by the news and no longer wanted to continue with their work.

We had to make changes. All the members of the radio station's board of directors were being persecuted. All of us who worked with the radio had to leave town for fear of the threats. We sensed that a wave of violence had started. We saw more violence almost every day. It no longer felt safe to continue living in town. Many people had to leave in search of refuge.

The radio station closed after the military came in to take our equipment. Later some people came in to steal anything that was left. The military brought a truck to take a lot of things we had in the offices—equipment, microphones, office machines. The radio station building is inside of town, so the neighbors saw that the offices were open, and some of them came in to take what was left over. At that the radio station was entirely closed.

The kidnappings were hard. People could no longer carry on with their lives or hold meetings. We waited a few weeks or months and then began to return to our families, without meeting as a board of directors. I dedicated myself to doing my own work, staying at home and weaving.

I was working at home when Padre Apla's came to my house to tell me that he wanted to open the radio again. "I want to open the radio to talk to the people and resume the work that the station has been doing. The radio was doing a very good job, and for that reason I am going to look for people to start the radio again," he told me. This was a few months after it had been closed, in January or February 1981.

Reopening would not be easy. First, we would have to reinforce the doors with iron and restore everything inside. When people had looted the building, they had painted both army and guerrilla graffiti on the stones and walls. Father Stanley entered the building and found equipment lying around—some consoles and turntables—and took it back to the parish. We still lacked the necessary equipment to start transmitting again.

I told Father Stanley, "Be careful, Father, because they are not going to like the fact that we are still communicating with the people. They do not understand the work we are doing in education here." I told him that I thought we should wait. The radio station is a work of social communication for the good of the communities. Programing goes out on our frequency to other communities, municipalities, and departments of the country. It is not only here.

"Soon, then," Father Stanley said. "I am going to do my best to make it happen. Just tell me where the legal papers for the station are, along with documentation of the frequency." The problem was, we had kept this in the station files, but the files had been trashed—all the paper thrown on the radio floor. We had tried to save what we could. But we didn't know what had been found. Still, Father Stanley did what he could, fixing the doors and windows with metal. To this day the building remains, with these repairs.

## ARRESTED

After the killing of Padre Apla's, the military commissioners used his death as a pretext to interrogate other people. They wanted someone to take the blame. I was eventually picked up. They also blamed Mother Maria de San Pedro and a nurse from the Philippines named Berta, who was working at the health center and living in the parish. They took down my name and wanted to implicate me in what had happened. From then on, I really suffered. They came to my house a number of times, searching for me.

In 1981, after Father Stanley's death, more or less in September or October, the military commissioners took me to the base in Canton Panabaj, near the edge of Santiago. They detained me and accused me of having continued to run the radio station, even though I had resigned. They wanted me to tell them everything that had happened here in Atitlán. I told them that I was willing, that we had nothing to hide. But they told me that I had to remain detained on the base for a few days. I didn't have any choice.

While I was on the base, three officers began to interrogate me. They asked me what I was doing, what other work we were doing, and what work the association was doing. I explained to them about education, literacy, health, and the different programming we had on the radio. I had to talk with them, to tell the truth, and say how many colleagues and workers we had in each municipality. But I insisted, "There is nothing illegal in any of this. We are working according to the law, because the radio station has a license to operate as a combined radio and school." I was held at the base for 15 days.

Eventually I told them that, if they were going to keep holding me, I wanted to talk to the Minister of Defense to be able to tell them what our work was and what our objective was. The colonel who was responsible for me agreed and said yes. The generals came—about 20 senior officers—to listen to me. They sat in a semicircle around me. They questioned me. I insisted that we were not fighting anything with anybody. We were only working on education.

At the same time, I also said some harsh things by way of criticism against them: "Look, we Tz'utujil manufacture our own shirts and our pants in our own families. Local cobblers make our sandals. Our dress is all made here in Santiago. We don't have to import our clothes. Even the moonshine we drink is not from abroad. It is not wine or some other expensive liquor. It comes from right here, made by local people themselves. So why fight with you? Why are we a threat? Why do our fellow citizens kidnap or kill us? Meanwhile, here in your headquarters you have all kinds of imported things. We don't know where they come from. We don't live like you do, so we must have a dialogue."

Most of all, I told them, "What we don't want is to see dead people and all the other abuse." And I left them with a warning: "If the people keep facing these problems, then someday the people really will rise up. Because we, as Maya, want to live in peace. Please remember that. Let us work and let the people work. I know we don't have jobs on big estates, but we do everything we can to earn our living, to support our families."

So that is how it happened. I could hear the screams of other people who were suffering a lot on the base, but they did not torture me. To tell the truth, my treatment there was more psychological. You get scared when you stay on a military base against your will. I had never been in that kind of place. The food was okay. But I didn't sleep well. They left me in a place to sleep on a rough blanket, on top of some coffee branches they had cut, and I slept there. I couldn't really sleep, but there I was, on blankets on top of branches. It was very cold, but I managed. I was well guarded. I could not move. I don't want to complain, because at least they didn't beat or torture me. They gave me food. Every two or three days the colonel would talk to me alone, asking questions.

It was certainly hard for my family. When my dad went to the base to ask about me, saying the family didn't know where I was, my dad cried. They denied that I was there on the base. For that reason, my poor father was very sad. Some of my cousins and a brother-in-law had been kidnapped. But with courage and faith in God, I felt that I had to dialogue with the military, looking for a way for us to understand each other. I believe that this is how I was able to continue living. They knew the reputation and respect that the radio station enjoyed in the town and that the people were with us. I think that is also partly why I was able to survive. It was a little harder for them to come down hard on me, because they were afraid of the repercussions. I was helped by the respect that the community had for the radio. Thank God. I survived.

After 13 or 14 days, they brought my companions Diego Reanda and Juan Tiney to the base. Then two days later they let us out. A lot of people were really surprised, because everyone thought we were already dead. They were grieving and missed us, since the community did not really expect us to make it. People were used to hearing our voice on the radio. And there was no more radio. There was no activity. Everything was sad. No music of our own. When we got out, people were surprised. One old man who had been grieving for us said to me, "Wow, I'm startled. It's like I'm seeing dead people, walking around alive!"


## IN FATHER STANLEY'S SPIRIT

Our experience on the base was frightening and sad, but fear did not hold us back. In fact, upon our release from detention we were encouraged and told our colleagues, "We have to open the radio, because it serves to educate the people." We began to talk and discuss this. I told my associates, "Look, Father Stanley wanted to open the radio station again." A few days after being released, we began to organize.

And off we went again. We voluntarily went a few days later to the detachment to ask and tell them, "Open the radio station for us." We were able do so, and we set to work. Eventually we went all the way to Guatemala City to meet with the Ministry of Defense, in the presidential office of a member of the governing board; I don't remember his name anymore. We went, and they authorized us. They wrote a letter immediately. It came with three or four signatures from the other higher-ups, the real authorities.

They promised that we could continue to broadcast, with all our programs. The military commissioners in our area of Atitlán continued to accuse us of doing something wrong. Before God, we had to speak out to say that their accusations were lies. We had to tell them to let us work and allow us to help the community. Little by little we presented our work plan, radio programs, and social programs, until they allowed us to proceed.

From there, we brought technicians from another radio station to help us. I went to ask them because I knew the people who worked at TGW radio. I went to ask them for help to get the station on the air for free. It was a matter of making arrangements and thanking them. In a few months we got other materials. We went to get some equipment that the bishop had in storage, because Father Stanley had sent it to the bishop of Sololá in Panajachel. Once we had our license back, we went to bring the devices, pick them up, and make them work again.

When people heard the radio again, after so long, they cried tears of joy. The radio station had been off the air for a year, entirely closed. A year later it was back, in 1982 in the month of May. But there were changes in the work. The literacy promoters who had been with us before did not want to come back again. There were only a few of us—about 10 to 15 people—who started working and doing activities. We first opened a center for "precious children," children who are sick, who cannot walk on their own, are blind, are lame, or have other handicaps. So that is how we started back to work following the death of Father Stanley. We also began to work on integral cultural education—with a little school.

At the end of 1981, the radio station's board of directors had again appointed me director, asking me to go to work and manage it, doing everything possible to clarify that we had done nothing wrong, that we had worked in social education and integral education. I didn't really want to, but the situation was very delicate. So I told them, "Okay. I will accept the position and do my best."

That is how we began to grow again. At the beginning, people from other municipalities did not want to collaborate, because they were quite scared. After all, many of our associates had been kidnapped and lost. But they did listen to us through the programs we launched. We opened more programs from five in the morning until ten at night, including religious programs, sports programs, and transmissions from other municipalities. There were always activities that people needed, in health, in agriculture, in religion—transmission of masses, children's programs, women's programs, countless youth programs, and indigenous music.

In this way, little by little, people were encouraged to collaborate with the radio again. Although Father Stanley could not open the radio station again himself, he had inspired us and, I believe, helped us to fulfill his wish. We fought for Father Stanley's word to be fulfilled, to reopen the radio station, to not give up or leave it off the air.

## GENERAL REFLECTION

The life we had to live in these years was hard. It was not just, and it was not Christian. War did not leave us anything good. Rather, it left us with poverty and suffering—children, girls, women, young ladies, old people, and men, all frightened and crying. We could no longer work. We could no longer go outside the village to the fields. There were so many accusations. It left me with a strong and abiding pain. To live through such a time was to suffer.

As Maya people, we know that we have a language, a history, and the examples of ancestors who lived by helping each other. In contrast, the repression afflicted us with more poverty and suspicion within the community. Already we did not have enough land, homes, or health—and then they treated us that way? I believe this treatment was a sin before God. For me the person or persons who direct the policies of each nation should think how to govern in a more humane way. They should administer through dialogue, doing everything possible to find how and in what way to treat a community appropriately, not by leading us to kill each other, as they did in the 1980s.

That is not the way. Taking the life of another person is not the solution to the problems of any community. As I have said, there are vulnerable children and elderly people in our communities. It was so sad and so painful. It is all well and good that humanity is discovering the moon and other planets, but we are neglecting our own planet and the beautiful creatures that are our fellow humans or our relatives in nature.

Our duty is to make the work easier, to be better brothers and sisters, to be better friends, to understand our life situations, to shake hands both from above and from below. Learning to work and support a family is a wonderful thing. Many people, many boys and girls, are intelligent, but they don't have a chance in life. Why don't we give skills to these children? Once they grow in capacity, young people can start working too.

It is true that our society has enjoyed development, but what kind of development? If we look around now, we see many people who once did not wear shoes or even sandals. Before, some could not even buy sandals. How many people once did not have glasses! How many people did not have imported clothes! Now lots of people are involved in commerce, buying here and there. Everyone at least wears sandals. They buy radios, they buy televisions. But these products are all made in other countries. And we still lack the kind of development that helps us get to know each other as friends, not treating anyone as inferior or superior.

It is wonderful to have a loaf of bread and be able to give to five or six other people, to live the life as God asks of us. That is where Jesus' message comes in, the message that no one owns the whole world. I believe that God left us the world for us to work in and to sustain a family, sowing what we want. But not by fighting, not by destroying the world. If we want to live in a peaceful way, we must dialogue. By dialoguing, we come to understand things. That is what I feel most deeply. It is in my heart to insist on this, based on all my painful experiences. I hope we don't return to those evil thoughts and attitudes toward our fellow humans, but rather, that we will forgive each other.

Ever since I was young, I have said how good it is to collaborate with people, how good it is to help others, how good it is to teach what we have learned. But as we lived through the time of massacres, kidnappings, and so much abuse, with people accusing each other, there came a certain moment when I despaired. I thought, "I think it would have been better if I had not gotten involved in social action projects." That's what I thought for a while. Because there are moments when one is disconsolate. There was a moment when I was alone, regretful, like St. Peter the Apostle. They took his master and he said, "No, he is not my master." I went through experiences like that for a time.

Nonetheless, after I returned to my position at the radio station, I had to recommit my life. "If God has chosen me," I said, "then I am willing to accompany the communities. If possible, we are going to rebuild our organization." We also started up the center for precious children, thanks to the support of the teachers, nurses, and advisors to our program. Once I woke up, I recognized other challenges and thought about how we could help and work. Throughout my life, I have always loved working in education, helping young people and children in one way or another. So I continued my work.

I keep active. Now that I'm this age, I'm trying to find something new I can do to be of service. Enemies are never entirely absent. They follow any good work. In other words, evil is always around. But thank God for the encouragement that Father Stanley left us to start up the radio station again. He is still encouraging us. If he could not start it again himself, because he died, we had to be the ones to start it again. That was his wish. The love and the vision that he showed us are still alive—resurrected—and we must never let the voice of our shepherd die.

Juan Ajtzip in front of the Peace Park in Panabaj Canton, Santiago Atitlán. (Photo by Gerald Schlabach.)

# CHAPTER 9

# The assassination

I HAVE HIGHLIGHTED FATHER Stanley's identification with the Tz'utujil people of Santiago Atitlán, but there was a cost, which we now know well. It was very rare for a North American to speak a Mayan language better than Spanish, as did Blessed Padre Apla's. Along with his dedication to the needs of the poor, this signaled the depth of his identification with the indigenous people, at a time in history when it easily attracted suspicion. After all, the military authorities feared that the Maya were being recruited by the guerrillas or by progressive priests. I believe that Father Stanley survived as long as he did in the midst of these growing tensions thanks to his integrity and his evident pastoral heart. But that time ran out.

## "I'M NOT LEAVING"

Father Stanley was moved by his affection, his love, and his dedication to the community. If you look at some of the photos taken at that time, you can see that he spent much of his time with the elderly and with children, and that he loved them very much. For me, what was impressive was his total dedication to the community. God had chosen him, had appointed him, to be the pastor of this people. Truly, it was so.

Padre Apla's gave himself totally. He didn't care about the threats. He said he was not going to leave; he was not going to another country until the problems were totally over. He was going to continue serving the community. He understood that it is not God's will for any person to take the life of another. Thus, with the love that he was living out among the people, and with his understanding of Tz'utujil, he kept that very strong commitment by which he had entered into our culture. It reflected the dedication by which he had given himself, before God, to love and serve his neighbor.

He had encountered all that the Maya faced in Guatemala, palpably touching our problems. With his presence, accompanying his church by helping the sick, the youth, the children, in education, in sports, in religious matters, and much more as well, he touched the deepest needs of the people. As tensions rose, therefore, he responded by assuring us, "How can I leave you? No, I am going to continue among you, precisely because the problems run deeper than ever, and it is the responsibility of a pastor. It cannot be that when there is a problem I leave quickly. No, it is when a challenge arises that my commitment to you grows, so that I can accompany you as far as possible."

That is why, although he went back to his country for a few months in early 1981, he quickly returned. His bishop did not want him to return to Guatemala, because of the danger, but he convinced the bishop that his conscience and his love for the Atiteco people were weighing on him and he had to return. What the people in Santiago were living through had gotten into his head and penetrated his heart. He knew quite well that the political and military problems were getting worse at the national level. Nonetheless, he told us, he was not going to leave. Father Stanley steadfastly remained with the church, celebrating mass, shepherding the people, and attending to social action projects. In fact, despite the danger, he began to give refuge in the church to young people and others who were being threatened.

Instead of leaving, he celebrated mass more often. He led more prayers. He cried for the people. He cried for the children, for the elderly, and for all the suffering people—those who had economic problems at work, in the family, in their homes. At the moment when the people confronted a very hard problem, he committed himself to help them even more.

I witnessed this commitment when Father Stanley came to my house to talk about reopening the radio station. He was concerned that we not lose all the effort we had invested. But I could not help but notice how sad he looked. He was so sad. Still, he was not afraid to walk about the village. No one accompanied him. He walked alone despite the danger.

Providing lodging at the church for young people and others who were in danger brought accusations. Those who wished to stain the name of Father Stanley accused him of subversion. But in truth, as a priest he did not belong to any ideology; he had a clear concept of what it meant to be a priest and to become a true Christian. The young people who had taken refuge in the church asked to take advantage of the opportunity to receive catechesis for marriage, baptism, first communions, and confirmation. Meanwhile, he preached as clearly as ever that none of us has the right to take other people's lives. How could a priest like him get mixed up in any cause that contradicted that teaching?

Still, there were many accusations. If we were to interview the people right now, years later, we would find a few who still accuse Father Stanley. They accuse him of many things, but in truth, he helped the population as much as he could, with all that he had. He could not take care of each one of the thousands of people in the town. Obviously he could not support them completely, because he did not have all the necessary funds. But with what funds he had received from outside, and with alms from the parish of Atitlán itself, he helped as much as he could.

There is a large population here and around the lakeshore, in all the other municipalities. They came to the Hospitalito and the Nutrition Center. They too struggled to maintain themselves with what funds were available. It was not possible to do everything. Nonetheless, the priestly charism requires a total dedication, with heart, soul, and a will to fulfill God's command to serve your neighbor.

I believe that Blessed Father Stanley—Beato Padre Apla's—fulfilled God's calling because he served the people totally. Even when other people disliked him or wanted to see him in a bad light, he did not listen to them. Say what they would, he kept on working. He kept on walking about in all the neighborhoods, helping people, celebrating mass and prayers, baptisms, and marriages. He walked without protection. He walked alone, talking to the people.

## AMONG THE PEOPLE

In spite of Father Stanley's clear pastoral outreach, some thought that he was helping the guerrillas in the mountains. There were many accusations against him for helping the poorest of the people. They misunderstood him, more than anything else. As a result, they killed him.

It is such a shame that in our country the very leaders who could lead us to peace were the ones accused. Their supposed sin was to seek the development of the people, to help people in need. That was the hardest and most tragic moment, resulting in the loss of the life of such a beloved pastor.

Still, I am always very grateful to God to find men and women who wish for, and think about, the development of the people. In addition to

Father Stanley, I think of Monsignor Gregory Schaffer, who worked for some fifty years in San Lucas Tolimán, across the lake. He had a very good relationship with Father Stanley. The two supported each other and learned a lot from each other, in terms of how to work with the people. The fact that Monsignor Gregory asked to be buried in San Lucas Tolimán among the people he loved so much is a great sign of his commitment. Father John Goggin, Monsignor Gregory's colleague in San Lucas, was also an excellent person who continued to work there until his death in 2023. Because of his great faith in God, Father John worked in the most isolated plantations and villages.

For each of these men of God, the way to work was to live right among the people, sharing their daily bread. That is why Father Stanley did not abandon Atitlán. Other priests stayed for a while—about two or three years—and then they left. The other missionaries from Micatokla who were here were temporary, coming and going. Not Father Stanley. Not Monsignor Gregory. They are people who not only talked, not only went to mass, but really gave themselves to helping *los humildes,* the humble ones, both materially and spiritually. For me they are people who wanted the development of the people, who truly wanted to help the people.

## CRISIS POINT

Of course, Blessed Stanley Rother's dedication to the people did not diminish the danger. At some point, identifying with poor people in a practical way was going to attract attention, and with attention came accusations. In a village, not everyone thinks alike. If you do well, others look at you badly, even though we are living in the same situation. Even though we live through the same crisis, there is always another Judas out there to do bad for someone else, thus spreading recriminations.

What is clear to me is that Father Stanley fought for the welfare of the people with the ideas of the Gospel and under the mandate of the bishops, coordinating with the local bishop here and with his bishop in the United States. When he began to receive threats, he may have been told, "Come home. Get out of there. It's dangerous," and who knows what else. But he said, "No. Thank you. Here there is a need to accompany the people." And some were denouncing him, even at the international level.[1] But Padre Ap-

---

1. See Scaperlanda, *The Shepherd Who Didn't Run,* 201–3.

la's kept his commitment. Even when he traveled back north to the United States, he said, "I have a commitment with the people."

He was faithful even unto death. He did not begin to think, "I have to go back to my hometown. People are wealthier there. Maybe I can fulfill my priestly vows there, since I'm in danger here." He didn't say, "I have assets there. My parents can give me food, land, whatever I need." Instead, he said, "Here are my friends, my sisters and brothers. I have to fulfill my calling and work for them here." That's why we totally experienced Padre Apla's as a brother, or as a parent completely committed to his children and to the word of God. He fulfilled his commitment with the brothers and sisters of the church. We loved him very much.

The room in the parish priest's house where Blessed Father Stanley "Apla's" Rother was murdered, now converted into a chapel. (Photo by Gerald Schlabach.)

When Father Stanley was assassinated, the people in the church felt as if we had been dowsed in ice water. "Oh no! Why did they kill our priest? Why? He is the priest that God truly gave us. He has preached well. He has done so much to be a brother, to be a better and better friend, amid all the cultures of our people." The people wept bitterly. They felt this very strong feeling, as if a father had died in the family. Or a brother who was as committed as he could be.

It was not only Catholics who shared this sadness. His friends from other churches felt it too. As I have already said, Father Stanley did not help the members of the Catholic Church exclusively. He helped all the groups that had needs, seeking the good of all the people, working for development. He did not see differences. He did not say, "You are not Catholic, and I will not help you. You are sick because you are not a Catholic." He helped them all, without distinction. In turn, they felt the great pain of his death, without distinction.

## UNLESS A GRAIN OF WHEAT . . .

They thought it through: what part of his body should stay here, after his assassination. The people in Catholic Action and others asked that some part of his body be left here, although we really wanted his whole body to remain. The missionaries, archbishops, and bishops insisted that they had to take his body back to Oklahoma, although they agreed that a part of it could remain here. His blood and his heart represented the feeling that he had for the people, and we are happy that they will remain here in Santiago. His blood has been placed in a very nice place, under the altar, where they celebrate the daily mass, while his heart rests inside a monument at the entrance of the church.

Memorial near the entrance of the church of Santiago Apóstol in Santiago Atitlán, in which the heart and blood of Blessed Stanley "Apla's" Rother is buried. (Photo by Gerald Schlabach.)

When Padre Apla's was killed, the great sadness felt by the people spread, especially in the parish, because we no longer had a priest to attend the parish. We had been orphaned. But we give thanks, many thanks. We are very grateful for the services that the priests of San Lucas Tolimán gave to Santiago Atitlán, especially Monsignor Gregory Schaffer, Father John Goggin, and other missionaries who lived in San Lucas. They came to help the town in every possible way at the time of Father Stanley's death.

Then, after about three years, the archdiocese in Oklahoma sent another priest, Father Thomas McSherry. He came in 1984. He also began to work hard, and he was also an excellent priest for Santiago Atitlán. He too came with a vision of community development. He supported the same work that Father Stanley had begun, publishing the New Testament in Tz'utujil that Padre Apla's had started, and he emphasized the education of youth and children. He sought to recover what we had lost. He did a great job in forming groups in each neighborhood, organizing activities where the youth could participate. Just as Father Stanley had done, Father Thomas looked for a way to relate to the *cofradía* without any division.

At the same time, Father Thomas emphasized catechetical training, following through on the plans we had made in the parish, with baptisms, with marriage, with the children, with first communions. He organized the people into small groups in each community, with quality education, prioritizing activities to help the people in a more organized way. Thus the catechists became more organized with charitable activities. They call it charity because they have to look for ways to help the people in their neighborhood who are in need.

Father Thomas supported the activities of the parish by building centers for Catholic Action in each neighborhood and by building schools. There are a lot of things he did to support the development work. He also initiated the construction of the stone pavement on the plaza in front of the Catholic church, and a few years later in the construction of a park on the site where the government signed its document of peace. It was his idea that they celebrate mass there on the second of every month, after the signing of the peace agreement in Santiago.

This was all great for us, although after a few years, he had to leave. I think he too was threatened. But for us he was a great priest too. He stayed for 17 years, until 2001, doing a good job for Santiago. His work was also admirable, constantly accompanying and training his catechists with a very good pastoral plan.

## . . . FALLS INTO THE EARTH AND DIES . . .

Of what happened at the exact moments of the assassination, I cannot relate many details.[2] We were at home, sleeping with the family when we were told that Padre Apla's had been killed. Early in the morning they began to tell people the news. That's when we got up to go and see if it was true. Of course it was true, because they already had Father Stanley laid out in a coffin. That is when the tears fell very hard, very hard. All the people got up to look at him, to pray. I don't know how to recount all this, but it was a hard moment.

Who broke in? Only the perpetrators know exactly how they entered the parsonage. They entered like thieves. Those who were there in the parsonage have told and written something of what happened. On July 28, 1981, men entered the parsonage. They forced the security guard to tell them where to find Father Stanley sleeping. The guard did not want to say, but they forced him to lead them to his room. He called to the priest, saying that some men were looking for him. It is thought that, in order to protect the guard's life, Father Stanley opened the door. The men came in to kidnap him, but he fought to keep them from taking him. When they knew they could not take him, the men killed him with two bullets and ran out into the street screaming.

Only in this way did they succeed in killing Christ's apostle to us. They hated him because he loved his church so much with the love and justice of God and because of his love for his neighbor.

At the moment of his assassination I was at home, a few blocks away. We couldn't actually see how it happened. They said that he was there in his room. According to reports, he had changed where he slept in the parsonage, because he knew that at any moment he could be killed or kidnapped.

He needed to take care of himself. He and I had talked about the dangers when he came to my house to talk about his desire to open the radio station again. "Change your room," he told me. "Watch out for yourself. Be really careful. Don't go out on the street too much, because they are tracking us—you and me too." However, he still insisted that he was not afraid. "I have to go out and about," he said. "It gives me some protection to be a priest, and also to be a North American."

---

2. For details of the last days, hours, and minutes in the life of Blessed Father Stanley Rother, see Scaperlanda, *The Shepherd Who Didn't Run*, 25–27, 212–18.

In any case, Father Stanley was taking precautions. He decided not to go out at night anymore. He was on his guard, because he already felt that he was being watched by his enemies. He had told me that he wanted to change his bedroom, and he had done so. His room had been on the second floor, but he moved to another one. As I understand it, the assassins found him only because they threatened the security guard or someone else who took him to his room. To protect the staff, he had to show where he was; otherwise the intruders would kill them.

When we arrived at the church, Blessed Father Stanley had already died. His body was already in a coffin. Others had quickly put him in the coffin and put him in the church. A lot of people were praying, crying, saying their prayers, and everything—but everyone was grieving for him. The church was filled. The whole town was there. No one went out to work for the next few days—no one in the *whole* town! Partly it was because of grief, and partly because of fear.

Catholic Action took charge of preparing his body. Of course, they involved his family, the bishops, the priests, his parents, communicating directly to the States about what happened. The Archdiocese of Oklahoma took responsibility for arrangements. What we see now in the reliquaries of the church here in Santiago is his blood, and the monument with his buried heart—the heart because he loved us, loved us so much, and his blood because it is also the blood that he lived and that he shed among us.

## . . . BUT IF IT DIES, IT BEARS MUCH FRUIT

I remember when I was a young man working as a security guard in the parish in 1968 or 1969. Another young man came to me who was hoping to go to seminary. He wanted to be a priest. "That is my desire, to go to the seminary," he said. I asked him if he had inquired at the parish office. "No," he said, "I'm scared to go." "Well," I said, "then let's go together. I will go myself, with you and your dad."

We went to the parish and asked for Father Stanley. It was evening. He was working at night, still meeting with people. We went into his room, and he asked me, "What's up, Juan?" "Well, Father, sorry to bother you, but this young man wants to go to the seminary. He has reached sixth grade, but he wants to go to seminary. He wants to study. If it's God's will for his life, he wants to be a priest." Father Stanley greeted the young man in Tz'utujil, asking him about his interest. He asked him why he thought of becoming a priest, and the young man explained. Within a couple days, Father Stanley was trying to find out if there was room in the seminary. "Yes, indeed, there is," he was told.

The young man left, and he has been a priest for many years. In just this way, Father Stanley helped many seminarians who have now become priests. I have heard of some priests he helped who are now in San Pedro and elsewhere. He did a lot for them.

In fact, the grain of wheat that fell to earth continues to sprout. The example that Father Stanley left us continues to inspire our young people. Before the arrival of the Micatokla mission, there was not a single Tz'utujil priest. Now there are at least 12 Tz'utujil priests from this parish, as far as I know, and I trust in God that by the time this book comes out, there will be more.

# CHAPTER 10

# Conclusions

FIRST THEY SHUT DOWN the radio station. Then they killed Father Stanley. And the repression continued, leaving the town bleak and the population dejected. The state of fear made it difficult to work in the fields and walk in the streets. If you went out, you had to go home early. For example, I had to start looking for ways to work and support the family. I know how to work in weaving, and how to carve jasper, so I returned to do what work I could in my own house. But everything was subdued and sad.

It was a bit like St. Peter the Apostle after Jesus' death: "Well, we don't know what to do. Let's go fishing." Worse still, many of us believed—just as happened in the life of St. Peter—that we had to distance ourselves when we were accused: "You are also disciples of such and such a person." It is not that we denied Father Stanley and his teaching or biblical reflections. But like St. Peter we tried to stand back a bit.

After a time of reflection, though, we knew we must start again.

## SMALL RESURRECTIONS

Some colleagues and associates, those who used to work at the radio station, went back to work in the fields. They knew how to work in agriculture—planting coffee, harvesting coffee, avocado. They are very hardworking people. Still, we kept thinking about the fact that we had not done anything wrong to anyone—nothing at all! So we had to go on. That was the encouragement that Father Stanley's memory had left us, to start figuring out how to continue with the radio station again.

In any case, we had to make a living and support the common good in other ways. I got in touch with the public school system in 1983. The supervisor called and asked me if I wanted to work with them, working with the children in preprimary. He gave me the opportunity to take a test to get certified to work with the staff of the bilingual preschool. I accepted, because I needed work. They sent me to be evaluated for this kind of work. That is when I started working in Cerro de Oro. When I arrived there, I saw that there were many needs among the people.

Father Thomas McSherry also encouraged us. He was an excellent parish priest. I spent about 17 years as his translator in all his activities. I was also a communion minister with Father Thomas, collaborating in the parish with him. And as I have already mentioned, in May 1982 we relaunched the radio station, working with very few people, because there were fewer people willing to participate, due to the continuing threats.

Military control continued in Santiago Atitlán, and it was quite strong. We had lost many friends and colleagues in 1981. We had lost many people involved with the radio station. They were kidnapped, they were found lying on the roads. Or they went to Antigua to look for jobs and were found and disappeared or killed—some of the board of directors of the radio, for example.

Nonetheless, we refused to say that we were going to close the station again because of the dangers. We simply couldn't. We already had the resources to broadcast more than ever in Tz'utujil. Ever since the radio was born in 1966 with a literacy program, one of the objectives was to help our people read and write in Tz'utujil, in our own language. Thankfully, Father Stanley had launched a translation of the Bible, the lectionary, and various prayers. Father Stanley had hired a person to translate texts for the people to use. We used these texts on the radio. Since Father Stanley's death we have continued to use that Bible—everything that was already translated.

What was missing was for this Tz'utujil Bible to be published. But Father Thomas McSherry helped us. As of the early 1980s, the Tz'utujil New Testament had not been printed. It had only been translated. The manuscript had been left behind when Father Stanley died. So Father Thomas set about recovering the project. He sent the manuscript off to the printer. He was seeking to recover many projects after his arrival in 1984. He also initiated the reconstruction of the convent, paving the plaza in front of the Catholic church, and later the construction of the Peace Park.

When we started to broadcast again, we depended more than ever on the collaboration of the people. For example, we asked teachers to collaborate for free and work on programs. The staff at the station had to broadcast their programs, but then return to work at home. Those who went to work their fields came on the radio in the afternoons and evenings. After 1982 our network of community development projects was smaller, and fewer people participated. In the municipalities around Lake Atitlán, people took a break, although here in Santiago we did more collaborations directly in the community.

So we worked in various ways as we started up again, taking care of the precious children, for example. We had to find a way to solicit funds for the precious children's center. Father McSherry helped us in this project too, and also lent us a couple classrooms in front of the church. It was already a shared project. Everyone collaborated. It was not just the radio staff that got involved. We had only two or three announcers working directly at the radio station, but many others collaborated. We wanted the radio to belong to the people!

It was the people themselves who worked to create and broadcast the programs. That's how we saved the radio. We could not let the radio station die as long as we had the collaboration of the community. We felt that it is the people's radio, thanks to this collaboration. This is always our approach and the pattern of our work in our planning meetings. It is more evidence that the spirit of Padre Apla's is still with us.

Father Stanley had always been enthusiastic about mass communication as a valuable tool for sharing and living the Gospel. Indeed, people often phoned us to say, "Today in the hospital our relative is suffering and needs prayer," and then the prayers they asked for came out during the broadcast of the mass. Similarly, people who were not able to come regularly to mass, because of distance or bad roads or difficult circumstances, would ask us for help and to be included when mass was broadcast. Thus we communicated through our broadcasts with the villages and plantations, even when they were very remote. Some distant villages in the mountains are very happy because they can listen to the Voice of Atitlán. That is why Father Stanley had said that we must continue. And Monsignor Gregory Schaffer also asked us to broadcast masses from San Lucas Tolimán. He was very pleased when we started broadcasting from San Lucas every Sunday.

# IN THE MIDST OF CONTINUED REPRESSION

We continued working with the children, and I continued with the radio management until 1992. But during the 1980s, the continuing pressure from military control in our region left people feeling desperate. They really didn't like the restrictions by local commissioners that the military had imposed on the community.

After Father Stanley's death, we at the radio experienced constant harassment. Every two or three days a platoon from the army would arrive to ask about our programs. They would say that they had received a report that we were holding meetings in our building. The truth is that we were, but the meetings were classes to train our staff about broadcasting, or how to teach reading and writing in our own language. The military took advantage to control and watch us closely.

This type of surveillance was even stronger in the community. The soldiers stopped people when they left for work in the fields, carrying tortillas and water for their day. Soldiers would say, "Maybe you are taking food to people hiding in the mountains." We didn't experience a reprieve from the harassment until the miracle of 1990, when the people rose up without violence and won the peace agreement for our region [see chapter 1].

This means that during the whole decade of the 1980s, we lived in fear. In addition to the threats from the military, people also accused one another. One thing or another can always prompt a conflict between neighbors or relatives. This only increases when a whole community is living under pressure. Someone would say, "You are known. Your name is on a list. You are one of the guerrilla fighters," or things like that. They were lies that people told because they were scared.

I thank God that, with the staff of the radio station, we were able to face these challenges, in order to accompany and help the community. We found new ways for the station to work to help the poor. We started with an idea to raise funds for the common good. People gave their economic help to the radio, giving corn, beans, food, and clothes for the needy. Others then came to the radio station when they needed financial support for things like medical expenses. The community trusted the staff of the radio station to collect donations and deliver. We regularly announced how much we had raised and who had benefited. We were very clear that the radio did not keep any funds, that all we collected went to those in need.

In this way we avoided accusations that we were collecting for the guerrillas. We didn't collect in the dark. We announced, "So-and-so and so-and-so came to leave a certain quantity of corn or of beans." Then we called people to come to the lobby at the station and collect what they needed. Everything was done publicly, right there on the radio. People made requests and then picked up what they needed right there. No one could say that we were sending things up the road or out into the countryside. Everything was delivered right there, and the people received it right there.

If a person had an important need and needed to buy something urgently, we would announce it on the radio. We would even have them say it in their own voice. That way everyone had heard for themselves what the person said. We recorded their voice, and we repeated it over the air a few times. Then other people who were so moved came to leave their economic help. Later, we called the person who had received the help, and they spoke on the radio again: "Thank you very much, ladies and gentlemen of the town of Santiago for the support you gave." That was how we worked.

What we could not talk about frankly on the radio during those years was the kidnappings and deaths. Those responsible always acted with tactics that hid their responsibility. We could announce news of kidnappings and disappearances, but we could not blame anyone for the kidnappings. Of course there were kidnappings. People were disappeared. Or they showed up dead somewhere else. It went on like that. Everybody was scared, because nobody knew who would be kidnapped next, or who might be killed, or if it would be safe to go to the countryside to work!

Sometimes the firemen found the unfortunate ones dead and lying in the ravines. Who killed them? Who knows? Who gave the orders? Nobody would say. It was frightening to go to work and see people with their indigenous garb, lying dead along the road, with their hoe and knapsack. In the end, the relatives had to go to retrieve the fallen, accompanied by the authorities and firemen. Since we had never before experienced such awful things, people remained terrified.

After the national peace accords of 1996, both the United Nations and the Human Rights Office of the Archdiocese of Guatemala conducted historical studies on human rights violations during the civil war in our country. The archdiocese's final report, *Guatemala: Never Again!*, reports that nearly 90 percent of the violations were committed by the army, police, and groups affiliated with the government, while the responsibility of the guerrilla organizations was about 5 percent.[1] They had the data or the instruments to evaluate all these things.

1. REMHI, *Guatemala: Never Again! Recovery of Historical Memory Project: Official*

In contrast, though, we didn't have the means to assess who was doing what at the time. We didn't have the personnel to do an analysis or an investigation on this. We wouldn't have these means now, let alone during the time of violence itself. We could not assign responsibility publicly on the radio.

What has left me very sad in the years since our problems in Santiago began—I have spoken about this many times—is that situations like this are the reason there are international and national human rights organizations dedicated to getting out the facts. But their work remains on paper, it remains in books. No one reads or hears about it in our regions, in our towns, on the plantations, in the villages, in the hamlets. No one knows about what is happening.

And I'm not just talking about data. I mean the very human rights that people deserve. Women have rights. Children have rights. But it's only on paper, even as every child has the right to receive their daily bread. The child has the right to receive her education. The child has the right to receive the home he deserves. Children should not be working at a young age, instead of going to school. But many families cannot give their children an education, because they have no way to support themselves. So what has become of those rights that are written on sheets of paper?

The child needs a pencil, or a notebook, or shoes to go to school, but he doesn't even have sandals. The little girl goes around playing with stones, playing with sticks, making her own toys. That's why we see children with dirty faces playing in the dirt or playing with leaves of grass. She doesn't have anything else! So where are human rights these days? People sing. They shout. But nobody listens to them.

Think about the year when human rights were born in the United Nations, when so much started to be promulgated [1948]. What I would like to ask is why the proclamation of these rights still does not reach us. The people in charge—all the authorities who hold big positions—always figure out some way to relate among themselves, but in our communities, we don't hear anything. We gain little from all their talk and maneuvering. Who is for *us*?

Who advocated for us when I was a kid earning 10 to 15 cents a day to cut a hundredweight of coffee or cotton? And working on the coast, what did we eat there? *Tostaditas*, tortilla with salt, contaminated water. That's

Report, Human Rights Office, Archdiocese of Guatemala, foreword by Thomas Quigley (Maryknoll, NY: Orbis Books, 1999), 290.

why two or three months of work there leaves a person sick with malaria; you drink all the dirt that is in the river, and the disease attacks you. And how do we treat the illness? We take some herbal remedies and hope it will help. Where were the people who regulate human rights? Nowhere. Who speaks for these people who are sick? These people aren't planning clashes and wars; they are simply living in despair.

We who live in rural areas do not need handouts. What we need is a place to work. Let us work our fields, take care of our families, and don't bother us. Because we know how to work with handicrafts, to trade, or to plant our fruits, plant everything we need from the harvest of corn, beans, vegetables, avocado. The rural areas are the source of products that go on sale in the national market. If people do not work in the fields, there are no products in the market. If people do not work, and do not produce avocado or peaches, there are no products for sale in the terminal in Guatemala City. So, let's let the people work.

Others have written about these realities, researching and offering some analysis of what we are experiencing. But mostly, among the authorities, no one wants to listen. Or else they listen, but have no methods for offering solutions. At the national level, people prefer to remain silent.

## FINAL REFLECTION, FINAL CALL

The eras that we have had to live through were hard for us, both because of the poverty and because of the repression. It was not just a story that we heard, but something we lived, something palpable. We have heard of other missionaries—bishops, priests, and lay leaders both in Guatemala and around the world—who spoke about human rights and also lost their lives. It is a very sad situation, to live in this Latin America. Padre Apla's *did* listen to us. But his way of opening up and living with others (*convivencia*) is too rare.

Today we see many people who can no longer endure hunger or violence. They leave. They emigrate to other countries. They leave because they are afraid to live in a town where there is so much suffering, so much pain. Many go with their families. In other cases, the husband leaves, and the family remains home. Then the family is divided. Families start to break up. Parents leave their children. The children grow up, they remember their parents, but they are no longer together. When the parents return, they find their children have already grown up. Sometimes they don't come back at all.

This is a problem that really needs to be studied: Why is Latin America like this? How can we find a path of fraternity, without violence, without any kind of accusations, where people can work together peacefully in a country, respecting each other as children of God?

God loves us. Therefore, we must love our neighbor. We must love and respect nature, which is the source of all the wealth that gives us life and lets us make a living. Thank God that in this country there are many products that feed us. Really, I think that all we really need is to train people on how to cultivate more products so we can feed ourselves, without the need to import corn.

We the people know how to plant corn, beans, and other products. What is needed is land on which to plant. We don't need large plots of land. We need about 10 to 15 acres per family so that people can feed themselves, and mainly we need education.

But they don't listen to us.

# Glossary
## and notes on translation

*agave*—A plant native to arid regions of the Americas. Though it may be best known as the source of tequila and other liquors, it is also a source of fiber used for making rope, brushes, and mats.

*ajkuun*—Tz'utujil word for a traditional Maya spiritual leader, sometimes translated as a Maya priest, a Maya doctor, or a shaman.

*alfombra*—A carpet. To make a carpet means to express gratitude for a favor or a miracle to the figure that is being venerated. *Alfombras* are made with sawdust, dyed in different colors, most notably during the final days of Holy Week.

*Apla's*—Tz'utujil for Francisco or Francis. Since the Spanish equivalent to "Stanley" ("Estanislao") was hard to pronounce, Father Stanley Francis Rother became known by his middle name as "Padre Francisco" soon after moving to Santiago Atitlán in 1968. Eventually, people there began addressing him as "Padre Apla's." Note that the apostrophe here does not indicate possession, but rather indicates what linguists call a glottal stop, in which a speaker briefly shuts off air flow in the vocal tract. Though English speakers are usually not aware of making this sound, they do so, for example, in between the two syllables of the expression "uh-oh."

*Atiteco*—Someone from Santiago Atitlán and the surrounding area.

*atol*—A creamy beverage, traditionally made from corn and usually served hot, often with spices such as cinnamon, vanilla, coffee, or cacao.

*cabecera*—The traditional leader of the Tz'utujil Maya community in and around Santiago Atitlán. Although now largely ceremonial and displaced by the mayor in official government, a *cabecera* can still exercise moral power at key moments, as he did in the nonviolent uprising of 1990 (see chapter 1), acting in conjunction with the town's mayor and mayor elect.

*cacaste* (*kakaxte* in Tz'utujil)—In Guatemala and Mexico *cacaste* often refers to a wooden frame used for carrying loads on the back, using rope with a strap going up and around the forehead and thus efficiently distributing weight close to the body, parallel with the spine. Most often seen in Guatemala today by men carrying surprisingly large stacks of firewood.

*caites*—Sandals, especially traditional ones made from local materials.

*campesino*—Literally, a person from the *campo* or rural countryside, sometimes translated as "peasant." Because "peasant" is slightly pejorative and *campesino* is now fairly well known among English speakers, the Spanish word is retained without translation in this book.

*Catholic Action*—A Vatican-encouraged movement begun in the late nineteenth century in order to meet the challenge of anticlericalism by promoting greater participation by Catholic lay people in the Church, as well as Catholic influence on society. The Guatemalan church hierarchy established the first Catholic Action group in 1935, and within a few years the organization was playing a major role in the Santiago Apóstol parish in Santiago Atitlán, where today it has evolved into the parish council.

*chipilín*—A leafy green plant used in the cuisines of southern Mexico, Guatemala, and El Salvador.

*cofradía, cofrade*—Literally, *cofradía* means "confraternity," but because of the distinctive role that *cofradías* play in Santiago Atitlán and many other Guatemalan communities, the word is left untranslated in this book. A *cofrade*, in turn, is a member of a *cofradía*. With roots in late medieval Europe, a *cofradía* was a group of lay people initially organized by Catholic priests in order to strengthen Catholic faith and practice, often because of a shortage of parish priests. Today the *cofradías* are more closely identified with Maya practices.

*Convivencia, convivir* – Literally, *convivencia* simply means "living together," sharing life, or cohabitation, but it has taken on a rich meaning
in Latin American theology that is difficult to translate adequately.
Originally it referred to the experience of Christians, Jews, and
Muslims living together respectfully in medieval Spain. In Latin
American theology, it has also come to refer to the almost mysti-
cal experience of communitarian life, living and working together
in deep human relationship. Thus, even when context requires a
basic translation as "living / live together" or "collaboration / collaborate" or "accompaniment / accompany" or "working / work
together," the Spanish behind the translation simultaneously con-
veys the purposive communal dimensions of this life and work.
To remind readers of this deeper meaning, the text sometimes
provides the original Spanish in parentheses.

*costumbre, la costumbe*—Literally, custom, but used to refer to traditional
Maya rituals and spiritual practices.

*department*—For administrative purposes, Guatemala is divided into 22
departments. By way of comparison, departments are like small
US states and or Canadian provinces—or better, large counties.
Santiago Atitlán is in the Department of Sololá.

*finca*—Literally, a farm, but in Guatemala *fincas* almost always refer not to
quaint family farms, much less to small plots farmed by *campesinos*, but to large estates traditionally organized and managed in
a quasi-feudal fashion, though now sometimes in a more indus-
trialized fashion. Because these operations depend on low-paid
*campesino* labor, whether seasonal migrant labor or resident land
tenants, the word *finca* usually implies wide income or resource
disparities, with poor living conditions for workers who find it
difficult to escape cycles of poverty. It has thus seemed most accu-
rate to translate the word *finca* as "plantation." Also see *latifundio,
latifundismo*.

*huipil*—A loose, square-cut blouse for women in Guatemala and southern
Mexico, often woven and embroidered using colorful patterns distinctive to particular Maya towns and regions.

*integral evangelization*—Also known as wholistic (or holistic) evangelization. Refers to Christian action and proclamation of the Gospel that
seeks human social, economic, material, and spiritual betterment

in a way inspired by and *integrated* to reflect the fullness of Jesus' ministry and his proclamation of the Kingdom of God.

*Kakchiquel* – A Mayan language spoken in Guatemala, related to Tz'utujil and used to the east of the Santiago Atitlán region.

*ladino*—In Guatemala, the term *ladino* refers to a person of non-Maya or Hispanic culture. It does not necessarily correspond to the ethnic descent of the person. Someone of indigenous descent can become *ladino* if he or she leaves the indigenous culture behind. In Guatemala, the term does not indicate a Jewish identity or background, as in other Latin American countries and in Spain.

*latifundio, latifundismo*—A *latifundio* is the technical term for a *finca* (see above), a large agricultural estate run in a quasi-feudal manner, in a symbiotic relationship with *minifundios* (or sometimes *microfundios*)—tiny plots of land that are unable or barely able to sustain subsistence agriculture. This symbiotic relationship ensures that impoverished farmers must work seasonally and for low wages on the *latifundios*. The system as a whole is known as *latifundismo*. See chapters 2 and 6 for Juan Ajtzip's discussion of his participation as a seasonal worker during his youth.

*los humildes*—Literally, "the humble ones," in other words, the lowly or dispossessed who live in impoverished, often degrading conditions.

*maxán*—A native plant whose broad leaves are used in Guatemalan cooking to wrap ingredients before boiling. The best-known example in other countries would be tamales, but in the area of Santiago Atitlán the favorite is *patín* (see below).

*Máximon (Max-moon k'aam)*—The controversial personage or deity or idol or symbol of Tz'utujil resistance to the Spaniards, depending on one's religious or anthropological perspective in Santiago Atitlán. The wooden figure of Máximon, smoking a cigar and laden with neckties, resides in the house of a different *cofradía* leader for a year or more at a time. Carried on the shoulders of a *cofrade*, he follows the figure of Jesus carrying the cross during a portion of the Good Friday procession that begins and ends in front of the Catholic church. Whether Máximon had an authentic place in ancient Maya religious systems or is a postcolonial development is one of the many points of contention concerning him, as Juan Ajtzip discusses in chapter 7.

*meltïoox*—Tz'utujil word for thanks or thank you. Sometimes spelled *maltyoox* or *meltiyoox*.

*pacaya*—Palm flower clusters resembling elongated baby corn, with a slightly bitter taste.

*patín*—A favorite traditional food in the Santiago Atitlán area, in which meat or fish is placed on a *maxán*, covered in a tomato-based sauce, wrapped in the leaf, then boiled.

*precious children*—When the *Voz de Atitlán* radio station founded a center for the care and education of children with disabilities, they used this term to avoid the word *inválido* or "invalid."

*quetzal*—The Guatemalan national currency, named after the shy, magnificent, and endangered national bird of the country.

*tamalitos*—A food made of ground corn, similar to tamales, but smaller and without any additional filling.

*tostaditas*—Baked or fried tortillas on which a thin layer of other ingredients is placed, such as tomato sauce, beans, avocado, and cheese.

*la Violencia*—The somewhat euphemistic term that Guatemalans use for the period of genocidal repression mostly by the Guatemalan military and allied, clandestine, paramilitary groups during the country's long civil war. *La Violencia* peaked in the late 1970s and early 1980s, though it continued until the signing of the country's Peace Accords in 1996.

*xq'ajkoj*—Tz'utujil word for a wide cloth woven by hand by the women, containing Maya figures, and worn as a stole by *cofradía* members. When the *cofradía* gave one to Father Stanley Rother in gratitude for his friendship and work, it became one of his most prized possessions.

# Bibliography

Adams, Richard N. *Cultural Surveys of Panama—Nicaragua—El Salvador—Honduras*. Scientific Publications No. 33. Washington, DC: Pan American Sanitary Bureau of the World Health Association, 1957.

Brett, Donna Whitson, and Edward T. Brett. "The Tz'utujil Revolt." Chap. 2 in *Martyrs of Hope: Seven U.S. Missioners in Central America*, 35–42. Maryknoll, NY: Orbis Books, 2018.

Carlsen, Robert S. *The War for the Heart and Soul of a Highland Maya Town*. Rev. ed. Austin: University of Texas Press, 2011.

Christenson, Allen J. *Art and Society in a Highland Maya Community: The Altarpiece of Santiago Atitlán*. Austin: University of Texas Press, 2001.

Commission for Historical Clarification. *Guatemala: Memory of Silence: Tz'inil Na'Tab'Al*. Conclusions and Recommendations. Report for the United Nations Office of Project Services (UNOPS). Guatemala: Academy of Mayan Languages of Guatemala, 1999.

Flannery, Austin, OP, general editor. *Vatican Council II: Constitutions, Decrees, Declarations: The Basic Sixteen Documents*. A completely revised translation in inclusive language. Collegeville, MN: Liturgical Press, 2014.

Macleod, Morna. *Santiago Atitlán, ombligo del universo Tz'utujil: cosmovisión y ciudadanía*. Guatemala City: NOVIB, 2000.

Martínez Peláez, Severo. "The Ladino." In *The Guatemala Reader: History, Culture, Politics*, ed. Greg Grandin, Deborah Levenson, and Elizabeth Oglesby, 129–32. Durham, NC: Duke University Press, 2011.

Melville, Thomas and Marjorie. *Guatemala: The Politics of Land Ownership*. New York: The Free Press, 1971.

Murga Armas, Jorge. *Santiago Atitlán: organización comunitaria y seguridad de los habitantes*. In Spanish and Tz'utujil, Programa Sistema Penal y Derechos Humanos, ILANUD / Comisión Europea. Tz'utujil translation by Juan Vásquez Tuiz. Guatemala: Cholsamaj, 1997.

REMHI. *Guatemala: Never Again!* Recovery of Historical Memory Project: Official Report, Human Rights Office, Archdiocese of Guatemala. With a foreword by Thomas Quigley. Maryknoll, NY: Orbis Books, 1999.

Scaperlanda, María Ruiz. *The Shepherd Who Didn't Run: Father Stanley Rother, Martyr from Oklahoma.* Huntington, Indiana: Our Sunday Visitor Publishing Division, 2015.

Soto Paiz, Manlio. *Maximón y lo inconsciente colectivo: arquetipos y simbología.* Guatemala: Editorial Universitaria, 2018.

Stanzione, Vincent James. *Rituals of Sacrifice: Walking the Face of the Earth on the Sacred Path of the Sun: A Journey through the Tz'utujil Maya World of Santiago Atitlán.* Photography by Paul Harbaugh, illustrated by Angelika Bauer. Albuquerque: University of New Mexico Press, 2003.

Stanzione, Vincent James, and Angelika Bauer. *Los Nawales, the Ancient Ones: Merchants, Wives, and Lovers: The Creation Story of MaXimón.* Guatemala: Editorial Serviprensa S.A., 2016.

Thorsen, Jakob Egeris. "Modern and Orthodox: The Transformation of Christianity in Atitlan and the Marginalization of Maya Traditionalism." In "What is Human?" Theological Encounters with Anthropology, 403–30. Göttingen: Vandenhoeck & Ruprecht, 2016.

www.ingramcontent.com/pod-product-compliance
Lightning Source LLC
Chambersburg PA
CBHW071808090426
42737CB00012B/1994